OUTDOOR SURVIVAL SKILLS

LARRY DEAN OLSEN
Instructor, Outdoor Survival Courses
Division of Continuing Education
Brigham Young University

Published by the
Brigham Young University Press
Provo, Utah 84601

DEDICATION

To my good father, Dean M. Olsen, who has encouraged me in every way to follow wise counsel and to reflect a kind and respectful attitude toward nature's perfection.

ACKNOWLEDGMENTS

The very nature of presenting a publication based on personal experiences and training must, of course, involve the participants who shared those moments, so it is with deep love and appreciation that I acknowledge the following people:

My wife, Sherrel, who has cooked my meals for "many moons" on an open fire in many caves and under many open skies;

Lonny Paul Newman who accompanied me on some of the most severe tests of living off the land;

Jim L. Winder for his skills as a hunter and his endurance in testing with me some of the materials included herein;

Robert L. Burnham for his companionship and skills in primitive living experiences;

Norman Herrett of the Herrett Arts and Science Center in Twin Falls, Idaho, for his outstanding achievements in bringing to the public a form of education that makes the primitive mind live in the minds of people today and for his presentations of mathematics, physics, astronomy, music and the finer skills of primitive people which have inspired many concepts that are directly applicable in a primitive situation today;

Richard A. Olsen for his early example and teachings in the ways of a hunter and trapper;

Lucy Ann Olsen, my lovely sister, whose artistic talents are represented in some of the illustrations depicting edible plants;

Thomas A. James of the Department of Special Courses and Conferences at Brigham Young University who first encouraged me in the idea that outdoor survival should be offered in the education of all people and who has helped to see it made possible on the Brigham Young University campus;

Ronald C. Hills and Brent C. Dixon who worked directly with me in planning such a program;

The editorial staff of the Brigham Young University Publications for their work in editing and publishing this material.

Larry D. Olsen

ABOUT THE AUTHOR

Larry Dean Olsen, the son of Dean McKay and Lola Estella Olsen, was born in 1939 at Wendell, Idaho, and grew up in Jerome, Idaho. Early he became interested in his desert environment and the material culture of the ancient Indian inhabitants of the West. This interest led to an intensive study into primitive lifeways that has involved over nine years of research and experience. All aspects of primitive survival skills were tested by trekking into the remote canyon areas of the Western deserts and experiencing survival at its most primitive level. Living off the land under Stone Age conditions, using tools and weapons of stone and bone, digging roots and trapping game with primitive implements and traps, suffering cold nights without bedding, hot days without water or even shoes, and enjoying every minute of it, has given Mr. Olsen a unique concept of man in nature.

In 1958 he married Sherrell Lynn Eslinger of Jerome, Idaho, and in 1960 he graduated from Ricks College. He then served two years as principal and teacher at the Grandview School in the Aberdeen, Idaho, school district. His wife is a proficient cook over an open campfire and can turn out some excellent meals using only a pit oven and a flat rock for her kitchen. The Olsens' children share with them the life in the wilds and have been known to ask for second helpings of roast rockchuck and steamed crayfish along with mashed biscuitroot and tortillas made from wild sunflower seeds ground on a stone metate.

In 1966 Mr. Olsen began teaching classes in "Outdoor Survival" in the Division of Continuing Education of Brigham Young University, at Provo, Utah. His "cave man" approach to survival, based on the idea that survival training is best achieved by learning to live off the land without previously manufactured gear, has won wide approval. His lectures and wilderness laboratories have been valuable to all who have participated in them. Even the few who found it difficult to "eat to live rather than live to eat" gained a respect for nature and the way that man can be a part of it without having to depend on the elements of modern life. Mr. Olsen's mastery of primitive skills has made him confident that survival living need not be an ordeal once a person has learned to adjust to the plunge from the Space Age into the Stone Age.

In 1967 after completing a B.A. in education, he established a course in the Youth Leadership Department at BYU under the title "Youth Rehabilitation Through Outdoor Survival." This national award-winning course uses the stress of actual 26-day survival trips into the mountains and deserts of the West as a living experience for both the youth leaders and the youth who have joined the expeditions. The program has opened up a new area in survival training by providing a vehicle for youth leaders to help young men and women establish lasting values, to exercise courage in the face of seemingly insurmountable obstacles, and, above all, to develop a compassionate respect for human life and its relationship to nature.

TABLE OF CONTENTS

ILLUSTRATIONS

I

INTRODUCTION

At least once in life, every man, woman and child should know (1) the feeling of complete dependence on the bounties of nature, (2) hunger and hardship, (3) the meaning of total self-dependence, and (4) the personal inventiveness required to wrest a living from nature. Each should have the opportunity to learn the use of his own two hands in making necessary items for comfort and survival in nature.

Few of us ever depend upon our own skills and resources for our needs. We depend, instead, upon the manufactured items of our civilization to the extent that it would be nearly impossible to conceive of a life without them. We marvel at the ability of Stone Age people to survive under such adverse conditions as they were usually found. We envy somewhat their ability, and deep down inside of us we hold a secret fear that somehow, someday we may find ourselves in the same situation as these primitive folks. Even worse, we may find ourselves lost in a wilderness without food, water, shelter or even the know-how to provide them. We fear the thought of getting along without our "gadgets."

There has been much written on survival techniques in the wilderness. Most of it offers solutions involving previous preparation based on the use of modern gadgetry. Pocketknives, axes, plastic sheets and tin foil are minimum items in most survival gear. It is the purpose of this text to further reduce that minimum. It is felt that no man can truly learn self-sufficiency with a pocketknife in his hand. That knife is not the product of his own manufacture; therefore, in a way he is depending on the skill of someone else.

A person who can be trained to live off the land without the aid of a single previously manufactured item has gained a security unequaled in the realms of outdoor survival. This training is an outgrowth of personal development and must be achieved individually by actual practice. This text in no way attempts to develop fully all the aspects of complete survival but merely points out some of the more important techniques involved with manual skills and materials in living off the land.

It has often been said that "It is the little things that count." Much of the information included herein concerns little things like splitting bones and making deep notches in wood with stone tools. These simple, often forgotten skills can be most frustrating when the little tricks of making them easy have not been learned. Each item manufactured in a primitive situation requires much time and patience. A steel knife will slice off a willow in a second; a stone knife used on that same willow may prove to be a frustrating experience unless you know how to use it. Nature provides the Stone Age enthusiast with a few simple raw materials—basically, wood, stone, bone, animal tissues and plant fibers.

Fig. 1. Some people are always willing to learn and experiment with new and exciting things—even eating rattlesnake for the first time.

With these raw materials a man can produce every item necessary for his comfort and living—according to cave man standards! (Figure 1.)

The challenge of vaulting from the Space Age into the Stone Age may prove too great a shock for some people, and life is often lost because of inability to adjust. It has been the author's experience to witness the effects of this on many groups of people. The following case studies or "conditions" may illustrate the point:

Condition 1: I have taken many groups of boys into the wilds for survival training. Most boys seem to adjust—after a fashion—but some do not. One group of older boys from an average-sized Western town provided me with some interesting observations. I took a five-day trip with them into a semi-desert area of southern Idaho. It was early spring and the plant life was abundant. I killed several rockchucks for meat, and there was enough to fill everyone. Little of this abundance was eaten, however, because the boys suddenly became uninterested in eating. Even after the fourth day some of them were still fasting and in bad shape. As a matter of fact, one boy was afflicted with severe nosebleeds only at mealtimes and another constantly lay humped up clutching a blanket—his only contact with home. Neither of these two boys would have lasted more than a few days alone even though there was plenty of food and the weather was warm and comfortable. Why?

The answer lies in the fact that the mental adjustments required for eating strange foods and being deprived of the comforts of civilization were too great. These boys would have died amid plenty. Some of the following comments made were: "I could eat it if I *really* had to." "When I get home I'm going to buy 100 hamburgers and 10 milkshakes." "I wish we had a car to sit in." "When do we go home?" "I'd give a million dollars for a pocketknife." "I can't stand it any longer!" "I don't feel well." "Leave me alone!"

Had this been a real survival situation, these boys would not have lasted even beyond the second day. Panic would have taken over with complete exhaustion resulting. Such was the case with one boy on a trip into the Jarbridge area of southern Idaho. He became separated from his group, panicked, dropped his coat and pack, started running and soon exhausted himself. He had discarded everything he would have needed to survive the freezing December weather and was in a complete state of panic when we found him only minutes later.

Condition 2: The endurance of some people is particularly admirable when they remain calm even under severe conditions and exhibit a willingness to keep trying. Paul Newman of Sugar City, Idaho, is a good example of a boy that never gives up. The two of us were surviving in the Sevier Desert in central Utah. The ground was dry and hard, making

Fig. 2. We slept on a pile of grass under a tiny lean-to shelter.

root digging next to impossible. We each wore only a pair of levis and a light shirt. We had no bedding, shoes, nor implements of any kind other than a camera, pencils, and some paper.

After a few days we were pretty lean but still holding our own. We made sandals of juniper bark and slept on a pile of grass under a tiny lean-to shelter. (Figure 2.) Our food consisted of roots, a few seeds, cactus, and some mice, and living conditions were far more severe than those encountered by any of the group mentioned in *Condition 1*. Paul was ready every moment to try new things and never once turned up his nose at the food we ate. To the contrary, his enthusiasm was of eagerness to improve our condition while accepting what we had. This kind of determination makes a survival experience worthwhile.

I am reminded of the man who was alone in the middle of the desert with no water nor hat, one broken leg and no hope in sight. He had been crawling for days, and his hands were worn to the bone. Pausing to rest, he pulled himself up on one bruised and battered elbow and smiled at a dry bunch of grass saying, "You know, if this keeps up I might get discouraged."

One must love adversity to be successful in the art of living off the land. The challenges are inspiring and the rewards are satisfying. It is a real comfort just to know what to do should a real survival situation present itself. Knowledge of plant life and its uses, skills and techniques of working stone and bone, manufacturing many useful tools by hand and trying new and exciting foods are only a few of the rich rewards of learning to live off the land. Perhaps the greatest good that could come from the training is the satisfaction of being able to actually survive when lost or stranded in the wilds. There is one danger inherent with a successful bout with nature, however, and that is the likelihood that you may find it difficult to resist purposely becoming "lost" again.

SHELTER

The basis for shelter making depends upon both the need and the time elements. As a rule, all shelter building should follow the suggestions listed below; however, in special circumstances it may be necessary to throw up any kind of makeshift protection in a hurry to avoid getting wet or frozen on the spot. Even then that kind of building should never suffice. After a degree of comfort is achieved construction of a semi-permanent shelter will assure safety in the event conditions get worse.

Building for comfort requires more than a minimum of effort and calls for some sound planning. The basic rules to follow are:

1. Select a campsite that provides:
   a. Protection from the wind and storms.
   b. Protection from natural dangers such as flash floods, rock falls, high tides, poisonous plants and animals.
   c. An absence of insect pests (ants, mosquitoes, fleas, etc.).
   d. Enough level ground for a bed and fireplace.
   e. Availability of bed and shelter-making materials.
   f. An indefinite source of firewood.
   g. Food sources and drinking water near.
   h. Dry ground away from creek bottoms and green grassy areas. (It is better to sleep on dry sand to avoid dampness.)
2. Construct the shelter large enough to:
   a. Allow free movement around the fire.
   b. Provide space for a dry wood pile just inside the opening.
   c. Provide plenty of storage space for food and gear.
   d. Allow for a fair-sized fire pit for cooking and heating and enough space from walls and ceiling to prevent flames and sparks from catching in the thatch materials.
3. Construct the shelter strong enough to withstand high winds and heavy snowfalls. (There is nothing quite like having your shelter fall in on you at 3:00 a.m.)
   a. Use strong supporting poles and lash them firmly. (Most other poles and thatching can be laid on without lashing.)
   b. When using grass and boughs for thatching, always stack heavy branches against the finished lodge to prevent the wind from scattering it.
4. Use plenty of matting and grass for a floor covering.
   a. Keep it cleared at least one foot away from around the fire.
   b. Stir it up each evening or, even better, remove it completely from the shelter and respread it. (This is especially important in snake country.)
5. Build a good fire pit for heating and cooking.
   a. The pit should be at least eight inches deep and lined with stones.

    b. Spark protectors can be made by placing green pine boughs or upright sticks in a circle around the fire. (If they are at least six inches high, most popping sparks will be stopped.)

    c. The pit should be directly in line with the shelter entrance and slightly forward from the center. This allows more space at the back of the lodge.

Fig. 3. Desert lean-to made of sticks, juniper bark and brush. Tall grass and dry reeds serve as a mat for sleeping.

Simple Lean-to Shelters

These easy-to-build windbreaks are fine for summer living and if built sturdily will give ample protection in cold weather. (Figure 3.) However, they are to be considered only as temporary emergency shelters. A good wickiup takes only a little longer to build and is much more serviceable. The following points should be considered in constructing a lean-to:

    1. Be sure the structure provides protection from the prevailing *night* wind.

    2. Make a large reflector to obtain the maximum heat from the fire.

    3. A three-sided lean-to gives three times the protection.

Fig. 4. Wickiup with reflector fire.

Wickiup Shelters

This comfortable dwelling is one of the best. It provides protection from all sides and is easy to build. (Figure 4.) The construction techniques involve a three-pole tripod on which a tight circle of poles is stacked, forming a large tepee or cone-shaped frame. Over this frame is placed a thatching of grass, leaves, reeds, bark, rotten wood, pine boughs and even dirt. The entrance can be large and face the rising sun or it can be small for protection from all outside breezes. Using twenty-foot poles, a floor space fourteen feet across can be achieved. This allows sleeping space for eight people. (Figure 5.)

8

Fig. 5. Large wickiup built from dry poles, grass and brush which slept eight people comfortably during a severe rainstorm.

Rock Shelters

The favorite natural protection of the Indian people in the West was the rock shelter. This convenient shelter is simply an overhanging cliff or bank that affords protection from the elements. With a minimum of effort these shallow caves can be turned into first-class living quarters. In the winter, rock shelters facing south will catch the sun's warmth most of the day. (Figure 6.)

Low windbreaks or reflectors can be built across the front of the cave to give added protection. By leaning poles against the outside edge of the roof and thatching the same as a wickiup, a cave shelter can be completely sealed from the elements.

Insulated Wattle Work

It takes a little more time and patience to construct this type of shelter. Each wall is made by driving two parallel rows of stakes in the ground about a foot apart. Weave willow sticks along the stakes to form a fairly tight mesh, then stuff grass and other material between the two woven walls. The result is a thick insulated wall that will stop any cold. The roof is simply made of poles and willows with grass thatching piled on top. Heavy willow rods and brush piled on top of the grass will keep the wind from blowing it away. (Figure 7.)

Fig. 6. Rock shelters provide excellent protection from the elements.

Fig. 7. Insulated wattle work.

Sweat Lodge Shelter

The Navajo Indians make a small earth lodge for sweating purposes that also serves as a warm shelter. It is simply a small wickiup covered with a thick layer of dirt. It should be built over a pit large enough to accommodate at least one person and a fire hole. The earthen covering should seal off all areas where air might enter. The entrance is only large enough to crawl into and should have as tight a covering as possible. (Figures 8 and 9.)

To heat this shelter a large fire must be built outside the entrance and a lot of rocks heated. A small pit dug inside and to the left of the entrance serves as the heating pit. By reaching out the entrance with a set of wooden tongs, a hot rock can be picked out of the fire and pulled in, making sure that all the sparks and coals are shaken off. A single rock in the pit will heat the shelter for several hours. As it cools, it can be replaced by another from the hot bed of coals outside.

Fig. 8. Sweat lodge shelter.

Snow Shelters

Snow caves are the simplest to construct. They are dug into a snowbank that has a good crust. (Figure 10.) However convenient they might be, snow shelters are not generally warm. Well-made snow houses can be heated adequately but still require a lot of matting and floor covering for comfort. Lean-to shelters and wickiups covered with snow are excellent. (Figures 11 and 12.)

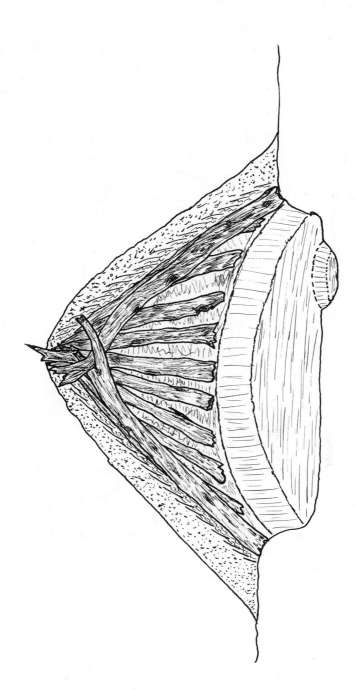

Fig. 9. Cross section of sweat lodge shelter.

12

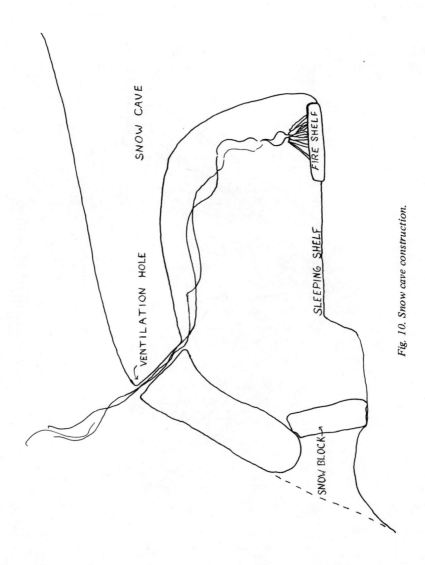

Fig. 10. Snow cave construction.

13

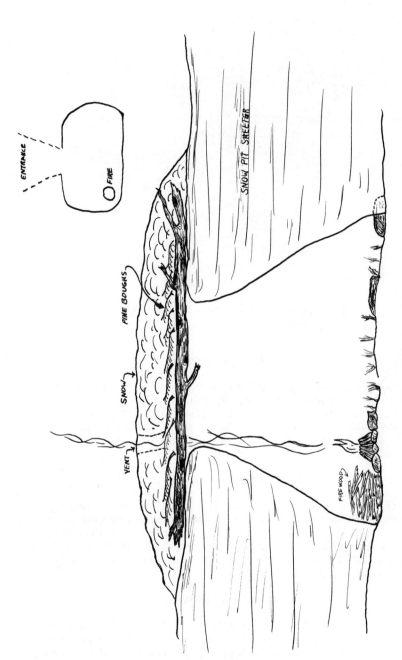

Fig. 11. Snow pit shelter.

14

*Fig. 12. Simple snow block shelter covered with blanket
with snow heaped on top.*

Matting and Bedding

Dry grass, pine boughs, juniper bark, cattail stalks, bulrushes and reeds make excellent bedding. They can be found any time of the year. Dry grass is found in the winter at the base of cliffs that face the south. Snow usually melts away in these areas and the sun keeps the grass dry. Cracks and small caves are usually stuffed with rat nests that contain enough grass for bedding.

Hot Pit Bed

Heating the ground under your bed makes even the coldest nights comfortable. When using this method, care should be taken not to allow direct contact with the hot stones. Even after several hours the rocks will burn holes in bedding. The stones are heated by building the fire right in the pit and then scraping out the ashes before the covering of dirt is applied. (Figure 13.)

Chimney Draft Bed

This complicated affair is a challenge to the good survivalist. Once built, it is unequaled for comfort while sleeping in cold weather. Such a bed is best constructed inside a large shelter or cave since little protection from wind and storm is provided. (Figure 14.)

15

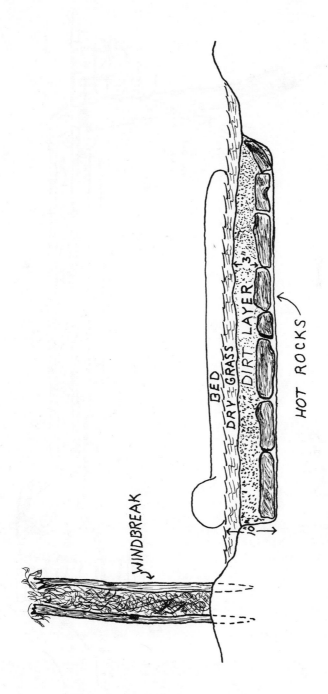

Fig. 13. Hot pit bed.

16

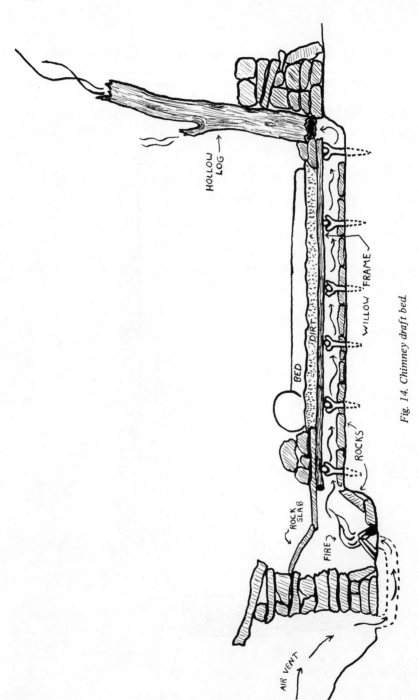

Fig. 14. Chimney draft bed.

III

FIRE

The importance of a good fire can hardly be underestimated. Even in warm weather a fire is important not only for warmth at night but for cooking, signaling, purifying water and aiding in the manufacture of various useful items. The following methods are inclusive and should be studied carefully. Reading how to start a fire without matches is one thing; doing it is quite another!

An inexperienced person should start early to prepare a fire. Then if he is lucky, it may be burning brightly by the middle of the night. This may seem a little harsh, but experience in watching others' attempts has proven the validity of the statement. The woodsman who can get a spark with seemingly little effort is either a skilled artisan or else he has made advance preparations.

The only way to become skillful in the art of making fire is to practice. If after hours of practice you are still unsuccessful and you have begun to see the futility of being an *amateur* fire maker, then it is time to make up your mind to be a *professional* fire maker. So wipe the sweat from your brow, reconsider your style and improve your equipment. Then practice some more. Once you have developed a style and have successfully started a fire or two you may rest assured that future attempts will be quickly rewarded.

Tinder

Good tinder can be made from most any dry bark which is light and fluffy. Bark which is tough and stiff can sometimes be pounded and rubbed between the hands until soft and serviceable. Shredded grass and dry moss, bird nests and various plant fibers can also be used. Finely shredded grass mixed with shredded cedar or sagebrush bark makes the best tinder. Small bundles wrapped in dry strips of bark can be carried easily for making successive fires.

Flint and Steel

Most sources list flint and steel as the easiest method of producing fires; however, getting a spark to "hold" is very difficult without the use of a specially prepared tinder which is not usually available in nature. Specially prepared tinder and steel are two items which may not be readily available in a survival situation.

The real secret to this process is to have a piece of previously burned cloth to catch the spark, although it is possible to start a fire with ordinary tinder which is very dry and fine. A miniature nest is made in the tinder bundle and the burned cloth is placed inside. A piece of hard stone, preferably quartz or agate, is held in the left hand and struck sharply with the closed blade of a pocket knife or other piece of steel. (Figures 15 and 16.) Considerable practice may be required to get good "hot" sparks.

18

Fig. 15. Striking a spark with flint and steel.

Fig. 16. The stone is struck sharply with the steel.

When a spark catches on the cloth, the tinder bundle is quickly picked up and folded lightly around the spark. By holding it above the head to keep the smoke from the eyes, it is gently blown with gradually increasing intensity until it bursts into flame. (Figure 17.)

Fig. 17. Blowing a spark into flame.

Bow Drill

Making a fire with a bow drill is a simple matter if the apparatus is constructed correctly. It has four parts: a fire-board, a drill, a socket and a bow. (Figure 18.)

The fire-board should be about one-half inch thick, and a splint from a dead branch of cottonwood is excellent. A slight depression must be drilled along one edge. This depression can be smoothed and deepened by a few turns of the bow and drill. A notch is cut in the side of the board so that it reaches to the center of the pit. This notch catches the fine powder ground off by the drill, and it is in this fine powder that the spark is formed.

The drill may be of the same wood as the fire-board, but it is often better if the wood is soft such as willow. It should be about twelve inches long and about three-quarters of an inch in diameter. The top end is sharpened to a point while the bottom is blunt.

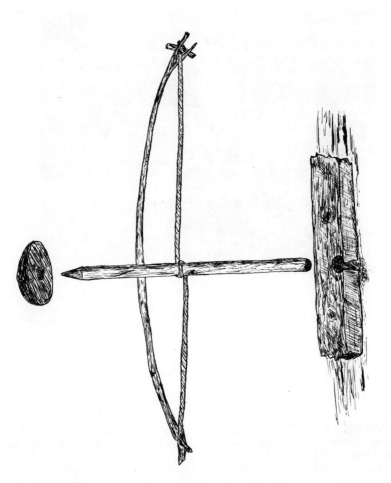

Fig. 18. Bow drill.

The socket is made by drilling a depression in any piece of hardwood that fits the hand. When in use, the drill runs smoother if the socket is lubricated with grease. Rubbing the top of the drill stick through the hair or on each side of the nose will give it enough lubrication. Using water to lubricate a wooden socket only makes it swell and bind.

The bow should be 18 to 25 inches long and about one-half inch in diameter. A branch with a fork on one end is excellent. The best string is a strip of one-quarter inch wide buckskin or other leather. Substitutes can be made from plant fibers, shoelaces or some other cord. The cord is attached to one end of the bow and twisted until it is tight and round before being tied to the other end. It is a good idea to fix one end in such a way that it may be loosened or tightened as needed. This can be accomplished by tying a small stick to one end of the cord and fixing it in the forked end of the bow. If the bow drill does not run smoothly, it may be that a little more twist in the cord is needed.

To use the bow drill the fire-board is placed on a flat piece of bark or wood. The spark will fall onto this piece and it can then be carried to the tinder. Another way is to dig a small depression under the fire-board and place the tinder in the hole in a position under the board so the spark will fall directly into it. The proper position for working the set is to get down on one knee and place one foot on the fire-board to hold it steady. The drill, with the bow cord twisted once around it, is placed in the fire-board socket. Using the hand socket to apply pressure, the bow is moved back and forth in a sawing motion with steady, even strokes until the drill tip is smoking well. Gradually the drill is spun faster and more pressure is applied with the hand socket. When a lot of black dust from the drill starts collecting in the notch and there is plenty of smoke, there should be enough heat for a spark. The drill is quickly lifted away and the black pile of dust in the notch is lightly fanned with the hand. If there is a spark, the pile will begin to glow, and then the spark is carefully placed in the tinder and blown into flame. (Figs. 19, 20, 21 and 22.)

Hand Drill

The basic principle of making a fire with a hand drill is the same as with the bow drill. Instead of using a bow and socket, the drill is simply twirled between the palms of the hands. The hands should be arched out stiffly for the best results. The drill should be at least 16 inches long or longer and tapered slightly from the bottom toward the top. Since this method is so difficult, it is not recommended as a sure way to get fire. Aboriginal people seem to have the skill necessary for this operation, but

22

Fig. 20. Fanning the spark in the pile of ground-off dust.

Fig. 19. Getting the spark with a bow drill.

23

Fig. 22. Blowing the spark into flame.

Fig. 21. Transferring the spark to the tinder pile.

Fig. 23. Using a hand drill for making a fire.

few "civilized" people ever achieve it even after much practice. (Figure 23.)

Other Methods

Various other less satisfactory techniques used to make fires include the fire saw, where two sticks are rubbed together in a notch until a spark is formed; the fire thong, where a strong vine or rope is pulled back and forth in a split stick; and optics, where a lens from a flashlight, glasses, field glasses, bottom of a pop bottle or a bottle filled with water is used to concentrate the rays of the sun.

Fig. 24. Fire bundles. The one on the right has been burning for six hours.

Maintaining a Fire

Once a fire is made certain precautions may be required to keep it going. When a person is camped in one spot for a period of time, a fire may be kept alive through the night by building up a deep bed of hot coals and banking them with ashes and a thin layer of dirt. The important thing is to keep the wind from the coals.

When traveling, tinder may be prepared by baking shredded bark until it is powder dry. It can then be carried in a dry container or wrapped in several strips of bark. The Piute Indians had an ingenious way of transporting live fires over long distances. They simply made a long bundle by placing a core of shredded cedar or other bark on several thicknesses of dry stripped bark. Additional layers were placed on top and the whole thing was wrapped tightly with more strips of bark. When finished, the fire-carrier looked like a giant cigar about two feet long and six inches in diameter. A hot coal was placed in one end and the Indian traveled with the fire-carrier in his hand or stuck in his belt. Such a bundle would hold a live spark from six to twelve hours. Usually two or three of these cigars were made and carried. When one burned low, the Indian stopped and built a small fire. In a few minutes he had a new supply of hot coals from which he would light another bundle. (Figures 24 and 25.)

Hints on Fires

1. A fire blower for stirring up dead fires can be made from any hollow stem. River cane and elderberry stems are excellent.
2. Use flames for boiling and baking; use coals for broiling and frying.
3. Split wood burns better than whole chunks.
4. Why chop a log when it will burn in two?
5. Soft woods give light.
6. Use reflectors for warmth.
7. Fire tongs save scorched fingers.

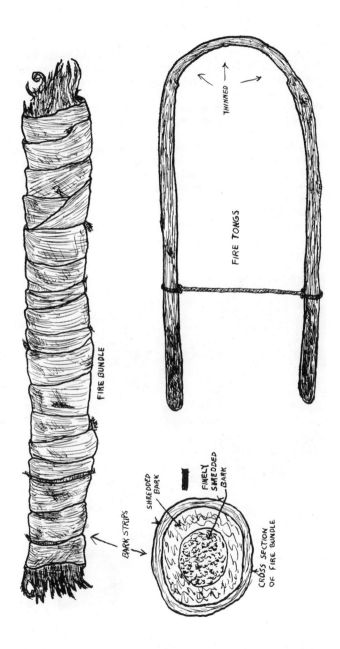

FIRE BUNDLE

BARK STRIPS

SHREDDED BARK

FINELY SHREDDED BARK

CROSS SECTION OF FIRE BUNDLE

FIRE TONGS

THINNED

Fig. 25. Composition of fire bundle.

IV

WATER

The Mountain West is often the scene for tragic experiences involving lack of water. With a little luck and training anyone should be able to provide himself with enough drinking water to stay alive. There are areas, however, that require special equipment if water is to be secured. Much of the dry desert area of the Great Basin is devoid of running water. The following pointers will help in locating water sources.

1. Dry mountain ranges usually have one steep escarpment while the other side is rather sloping. Most of the moisture will be found on the sloping side of these hills. The steep side has faster runoff and less ground area for the collection of water.
2. The water table is usually close to the surface and can be found by digging:
   a. At the base of cliffs and rocks where an abnormal amount of vegation is thriving. (Figure 26.)

Fig. 26. Water was found in drinkable quantities under this ledge at the bottom of a dry canyon.

Fig. 27. Digging for water in a damp gulley on the Sevier Desert of Utah.

b. In dry mud holes, sinks and riverbeds. The bends in riverbeds usually provide the easiest source of water. (Figures 27, 28 and 29.)

c. At the base of large sand dunes on the shady or steep sides.

d. Anywhere the ground is damp or muddy.

e. Where patches of salt grass, cattails, greasewood, willows or elderberries grow in low spots.

3. Old mineshafts and pits often contain water. Watch for ore dumps and tailings in the distance and head for them.

Getting Water from the Soil

1. Dig a hole in damp or muddy sink areas and let the water seep in.

2. Wring mud in a shirt or other cloth to force out the water.

3. Use an evaporation still. This new invention was developed by two American scientists, Dr. Ray D. Jackson and Dr. Cornelius H. M. van Bavel, of the U.S. Department of Agriculture. It requires some special equipment but is simple to construct. A sheet of six by six feet plastic (preferably Tedlar No. 100 BG-20 by DuPont), a plastic drinking tube and a container are all that are needed. These items can be included in a survival kit. The plastic sheet is stretched over a three-foot hole and

30

Fig. 28. Water was found at a depth of 14 inches.

Fig. 29. This simple hole supplied enough water for several people.

held in place with dirt. This seals the hole off from the outside air. A rock is placed in the center of the plastic to weigh it down until it comes to within about two inches of the bucket. The drinking tube is fastened in the bucket and extends outside the still. (Figure 30.)

Two of these stills in operation in even the driest deserts will produce enough water for one person each day. Placing green plants and sliced cactus in the pit will increase the amount of water. It is best to place the still in deep rich soil at the bottoms of gullies and in old riverbeds.

Collecting Water from the Air and from Plants

1. Mopping up dew. In many arid regions of the world primitive peoples supply themselves with water by arising before dawn to mop up the dew from rocks and plants. It is surprising how much dew can be found in the early morning in desert areas. The easiest way to gather it is to use a handkerchief or a shirt to gently mop it up and then wring it into a container. If a handkerchief or other cloth is not available, a handful of dry grass will do the job. It is possible to mop up almost a quart an hour using this method.
2. Many plants and trees contain enough water to allay thirst, but getting it is a problem. A cactus can be cut and peeled and the moisture sucked out. This is not like running water; rather it is more like trying to drink Elmer's glue. Larger cacti in the Southwest can be a good source of water when the top is cut off and the center pulp mashed and stirred with a stick. The pulp is then wrung to obtain the water.

   Some vines and green plants will help allay thirst when chewed and sucked but cannot be depended upon to sustain life. Trees at certain times of the year will yield a clear sap for drinking. The tree is tapped by drilling a hole about three inches deep and inserting a hollow stem. Maples, birch, aspen and white pine are the best trees and produce sap in drinkable quantities from February through April.

Some Precautions to Take in Using Water

1. If no water is available, do not eat anything because such eating uses up the body's water reserve.
2. Store water in your belly rather than your canteen. Men have died from dehydration with water still in their canteens.
3. Water polluted by animals or mud tastes bad but is harmless if boiled.
4. Muddy water can be partially cleared by allowing it to:
   a. Stand overnight.

32

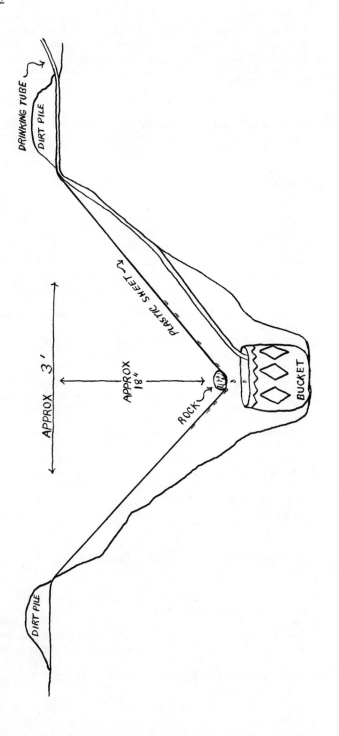

Fig. 30. Cross section of water still.

    b. Run through several thicknesses of cloth or through a grass filter.

    c. Seep through the bank into a hole dug about a foot away. When doing this for brackish or salty water, remove the top six inches of salty soil between the hole and the source of water.

5. Don't travel during the heat of the day and always walk slowly—never hurry.

6. Pebbles in the mouth, small sips of water, chewing gum, etc., may relieve thirst but do not stop dehydration.

7. Drinking blood or urine only increases dehydration of the body. It is better to soak clothing in urine to cool the body by evaporation.

V

PLANTS AS FOOD AND MEDICATION

The American West is certainly no Garden of Eden with respect to food plants. The variety offered is extensive enough, however, and anyone with a good understanding of harvesting and preparation methods may live indefinitely from plant resources.

It has been said that a person who can survive on the Great American Desert can survive anywhere in the world. There are areas that surpass the hot barren Sahara, the cold ruggedness of Mongolia and the jagged steepness of the Alps. In all of these conditions nature has provided adequately for the trained savage. The food quest is exacting and strenuous. Knowledge of the plant life is a must where so many edible species resemble poisonous ones. A careful study of these plants is perhaps the most important phase of outdoor training.

A Sermonette on Taste Buds

A certain amount of taste bud training is often necessary to make some of the plants palatable. This training comes from experimentation and mental determination. One should taste wild foods often and do it with a positive attitude. Many people die amid plenty simply because they cannot "stomach" wild foods. The stomach only reacts to the stimulus given by a prejudiced brain in these cases. A few people often develop mental defense mechanisms against eating. Profuse nosebleeds occurring only at mealtime, vomiting, headaches, lack of appetite and haughty indifferences are popular excuses for not eating. Needless to say, these defenses can kill even a healthy person lost in the wilds.

Harvesting Wild Food Plants

Digging Sticks

Finding an edible root is one thing; digging it out is another. Most wild roots grow deep and require special skill to get out. Skillfully applied, a simple device called a digging stick saves time and energy otherwise expended by scraping and grubbing with flat stones and fingers. The stick is made from a stave of hardwood about three feet long and one inch in diameter. After the bark is removed the stick is hardened in the fire. The tip is formed into a chisel shape by rubbing it on a coarse rock. For green wood to harden it takes about four or five scorchings in the fire to drive out the sap. Do not burn the wood. A good fire-hardened stick will be baked rather than charred.

Digging down to a tasty root involves moving a lot of dirt. It is easier to make the root come to you. This is done by pushing the stick down

Fig. 31. Digging salsify roots.

alongside the plant until it is even with or below the root. Then by slightly prying, but mostly by lifting, the root is flipped to the surface. (Figures 31 and 32.)

Seed Gathering

When seeds are ripe, they may be gathered in large quantities, using only a seed beater and a gathering basket. The seed beater is simply a small woven dish or ladle used to knock the ripened seeds from the plants. It should be dish shaped to catch and propel the seeds into the basket. The basket must be large enough to catch the seeds, yet small enough to hold in one arm. A shallow woven tray is ideal. A shirt held open with a willow hoop will work.

Plants that form large amounts of seeds in clusters such as red and Amaranth require only stripping with the hand to remove the seeds.

Fig. 32. Using the digging stick.

Flower seeds such as the nutritious sunflower *(Helianthus)* usually are beaten from the head with a seed beater. They can also be picked and the seeds rubbed from the heads on a flat stone. (Figure 33.)

Preparation Methods for Seeds

Seeds must be threshed and winnowed to remove most of the chaff and stems. This can be accomplished by beating them with sticks and then tossing them on a winnowing tray and letting the wind blow away the chaff. Reverting to this ancient method may seem quite harsh, but it is effective under limited conditions. Seeds may also be tossed in a blanket or tossed in the air from a pile on the ground. Using a blanket or tray saves much of it from being lost in the dirt. Small amounts may be winnowed by taking a handful and blowing away the chaff while pouring it from one hand to the other.

Fig. 33. Sunflower seeds can be threshed by rubbing the heads on a flat stone.

Most seeds are better when ground into flour or cracked for mush than when eaten whole. The technique of using grinding stones is important. A metate is most effective. This is a simple slab of rock that has been smoothed by pecking and crumbling. (See p. 138.) On the smoothed rock is placed a handful of dry seeds which are then ground with a mano or handstone. The handstone is a loaf-shaped rock with one flat side matching the surface of the metate. It is held in the hands and rubbed back and forth on the metate with a pounding-scraping motion achieved by a rocking action of the wrists. The arms should be stiff and the necessary weight applied from the shoulders. It is best to work with the metate lying on a blanket to avoid losing seeds that fall off the sides during the grinding process. Wet grinding may prove easier for some. Simply dampen the seeds until soft and grind into a dry paste. (Figure 34.)

Fig. 34. Grinding seeds on a metate with a handstone or mano.

Barks and Greens

Barks, leaves and stems should be stripped and picked with care taken to select only the young tender portions. They should be kept fresh and cool while gathering if possible. Do not soak them in water to keep them fresh.

Preparation of Roots

Flour from roots can be made by drying and grinding them on a metate in much the same manner as seeds. They may be roasted and eaten like baked potatoes or mashed on a metate for "mashed potatoes." Simple roasting, baking or boiling may be used for most roots unless leaching is necessary. Leaching of bitter greens, roots and nuts is done by boiling them in several changes of water or by pouring water through a bag of the mashed food. This process takes away much of the food value of plants and should only be used when bitterness is too strong for eating.

A steaming pit is the most effective way to cook roots and greens, as well as meat and other foods. A pit is lined with stones and a fire is built in it. After about an hour the coals are scraped out and the pit is lined with wet green grass. The food is placed on the grass and covered quickly with more wet grass. Then some water is poured on for steam and the pit and its contents should be quickly covered with a piece of cloth, canvas, hide, flat rocks or whatever is available to help keep out the dirt which is then heaped over the entire pit to seal in the steam. The food is allowed to cook in the pit for an hour or two. An advantage of preparing food in this manner is that its flavor and nutritional value are saved. (Figures 35, 36, 37, 38, 39 and 40.)

Fig. 35. Digging a cooking pit with a flat rock.

Fig. 37. Fire built in the pit heats the stones. Fire is scraped out after about an hour.

Fig. 36. Lining the pit with stones.

Fig. 39. More grass and a cover are placed over the food and a small amount of water is poured on.

Fig. 38. Green grass is placed over the hot stones and the food is placed on the grass bed.

Fig. 41. Amaranth.

Fig. 40. Whole pit is covered with a thick layer of dirt and left for about one and a half hours.

Roots and berries can be dried for future use. The roots are cooked and mashed into small flat cakes, then they are dried on flat rocks until hard. Berries must be partially dried and then mashed into cakes by pounding them on a mortar. They can be mixed with pounded meat for pemmican or dried in cakes. To use the dried cakes they must be broken up or ground and added to stew or soup.

Seeds may be dried or parched for preservation. Parching seeds is not difficult but requires a steady hand and a good parching tray. A tray may be made from willows woven closely to form a large shallow bowl. (A dishpan would work.) The bottom of the tray is covered with seeds and then a layer of hot hardwood coals is poured in. Next the tray is stirred and shaken until all the seeds are toasted. The coals can be removed by pouring the contents of the tray onto a flat rock and flipping away the hot coals.

Dried seeds, roots and berries can be safely stored in pits at the back of dry rock shelters and in crevices. A pit approximately two feet deep and lined with grass is sufficient. The dried food is placed in the pit and covered with dry sagebrush leaves and cedar bark. Over all this at least six inches of dirt is piled. A pit made in dry dust and soil under an overhanging ledge will remain dry for years. Insects and rodents rarely bother this type of cache.

Edible Wild Plants

The following list contains many of the more important food plants found in the Great Basin Plateau areas of the western United States. In this rugged section of America the plant life is rather restricted and in most cases adapted to arid conditions. The higher elevations produce more edible species which often range down into the desert valleys along stream courses. Edible seeds are the most common and comprise over half of the available species.

AMARANTH, *Amaranthus hybridus*

Description: Annual herbs resembling pigweed or lamb's quarters; scaly inflorescences; veiny, often hairy leaves and stems; seeds black, circular in outline and in clusters. (Figure 41.)

Uses: The seeds of this plant may be stripped from the stalk and winnowed for a delicious grain. Cooked whole as mush or ground for bread it is filling and nutritious. The young shoots and leaves make a superior potherb.

ARROWGRASS, Sourgrass, Goosegrass, *Triglochin maritima*

Description: A grass-like plant with a single stem that reaches a height of 1-3 feet. It is surrounded by basal leaves that look like grass stems. They are fleshy, rounded on one side and flat on the other. The upper portion

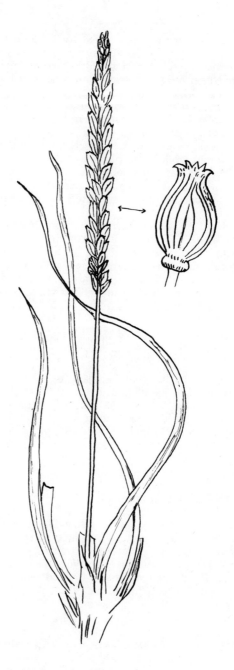

Fig. 42. Arrowgrass.

of the stem is covered with a spike of small greenish flowers. The mature seeds are rather oblong and ridged. (Figure 42.)

Uses: The seeds are parched and ground for food. The plant contains large amounts of hydrocyanic acid, making them poison if eaten raw. Roasting of the seeds eliminates the poison acid and renders the meal palatable.

ARROWHEAD, Wappato, *Sagittaria*

Description: Plants grow in water or marshes and are easily identified by their deep green arrowhead-shaped leaves that protrude from the water or lie flat like a lily pad. The stalk is a single stem with fruit bearing from lateral spikes in the form of round heads of flat seeds. The root fibers spread directly from the tuft of leaves and range some distance in the shallow mud from the parent plant. In the late fall small tubers form on the rootstalks. (Figure 43.)

Fig. 43. Arrowhead.

Uses: The small tubers, forming only in the late fall, can be gathered throughout the fall, winter and early spring. They are harvested by wading into the water and feeling in the mud with the toes or hands. Often large amounts can be harvested by raking the water and mud to a depth of about six inches with a forked stick. This breaks the tubers from the roots and they float to the surface. The only disadvantage to gathering arrowhead is that the weather is usually cold during the harvesting season and wading into ice water is not very pleasant.

The tubers are roasted or baked to remove the stinging properties, after which they taste similar to potatoes. They may be baked, mashed into cakes and dried for future use.

ARROWLEAF BALSAMROOT, Balsamroot, *Balsamorrhiza sagittata*

Description: A short plant with clumps of large arrowhead-shaped leaves and naked stems topped with yellow flowers. The leaves have a silvery appearance due to their covering of fine grey hairs. This plant is often confused with the short species of sunflowers, *Helianthus*. (Figure 44.)

Uses: The large root can be eaten after several washings and cookings to remove the bitter. The seeds and young leaves are edible in season, being the better parts of the plant. The root is often too tough and bitter for consumption in large quantities.

ASPARAGUS, *Asparagus officinalis*

The wild varieties are merely fugitives from cultivation and are often found far from human habitations. The stalks are a welcome change and a link with civilization for the trail-weary hiker. It is easily eaten raw or cooked.

BALL CACTUS, *Mammillaria*

Description: Cactus, rounded with central spine hooked, not grooved. The fruit is bright red and elongated. The entire plant is rather small and heavily spined.

Uses: Nearly all species of cactus are edible. Some "spotted" varieties are said to be toxic at certain times of the year. Cactus is prepared by burning off the spines and roasting the flesh in hot coals until done. The fruit is excellent food raw or cooked. To the uninitiated, cactus may be rather unpleasant because of its sticky nature. Some people say "It's like eating Elmer's glue. It sticks real good!"

BETONY, *Stachys palustris*

Description: A member of the mint family, this plant has the characteristic square stem but generally lacks the aromatic qualities of other mints. The stems are usually unbranched and the leaves grow directly from them rather than on radiating stalks.

Uses: The seeds are edible parched or roasted and ground into meal.

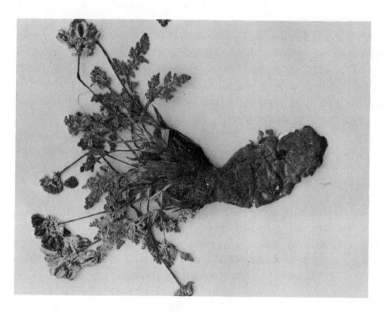

Fig. 45. Biscuitroot, Cymopterus bulbosus.

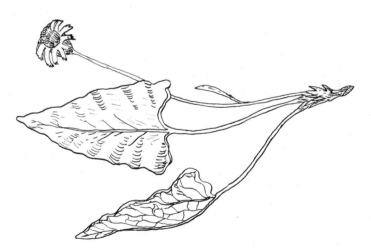

Fig. 44. Arrowleaf Balsamroot.

BISCUITROOT, Kouse, *Cymopterus bulbosus, Cymopterus longipes* or *Lomatium*

Description: Carrot or parsley family. There are several edible species of biscuitroot, some having slender rootstalks while others like *C. bulbosus* have swollen bulblike roots. The plants grow on hillsides and in rocky places throughout the West and are often found in quite arid places. The flowers are borne on compound umbels and the leaves are divided into narrow segments like carrot leaves. Care should be taken not to confuse it with related species usually growing in damp areas which are often poisonous. This family should be studied carefully to determine the various genera, some of which are deadly. One related specie, *Lomatium,* is also called biscuitroot and is used for food in the same way. (Figures 45 and 46.)

Uses: The seeds of some species are edible ground for mush or flour. The root is favored as an ingredient of stew and tastes something like dumplings. It may be boiled or roasted in a pit for the best results. The mashed root dried in cakes will keep indefinitely and was the famous "bread of cows" (kouse) so eagerly sought by Lewis and Clark.

BLAZING STAR, Stickleaf, *Mentzelia laevicaulis, Mentzelia albicaulis, Mentzelia dispersa* and other species

Description: A coarse branching plant one to three feet tall with beautiful yellow flowers and leaves covered with barbed hairs. The leaves are lance-shaped and because of the barbed hairs often stick to clothing. The edges are deeply cleft or pinnate. The root is deeply buried as opposed to similar looking plants with spreading root systems. (Figure 47.)

Uses: The seeds parched and ground into flour or meal make a serviceable food for mush and bread.

BLUEGRASS, *Poa* (western species)

Description: Grass common to rangeland. It bears wheatlike seeds in some species; others have spreading seed heads. It is not too important to distinguish between the various grasses as most all that bear harvestable seeds in a grainlike husk are edible. (Figure 48.)

Uses: The seeds harvested with a seed beater can be a good source of food when the season is right. Since most grass seeds drop shortly after maturity, the season is quite limited.

BRACKEN FERN, *Pteridium aquilinum*

Description: The most common of our ferns, being coarse and covered with felty hairs at the base. The young shoots uncurl in juicy stalks called

49

Fig. 47. *Blazing Star.*

Fig. 46. *Biscuitroot*, Cymopterus longipes.

fiddleheads because of their resemblance in shape to that instrument. The mature plant has a three-forked stem bearing the light green fronds. (Figure 49.)

Uses: Young fiddleheads have long been a popular potherb in many countries. They are best when cooked like asparagus or eaten raw with other foods. The mature fern is tough and unpalatable and may be toxic.

BROOMRAPE, *Orobanche*

Description: Broomrape is a root parasite found on many western plants. It has no green foilage and is usually a yellow or purple color. The leaves are simple alternate scales and the flowers are complete.

Uses: The roots of some species are swollen and make an important starchy food. They may be baked or boiled and mashed into cakes for storage.

BUFFALOBERRY, *Shepherdia argentea*

Description: Shrub or small tree; somewhat thorny with oval or nearly oval leaves. The small red berries last late into the fall.

Uses: The berries are edible and may be cooked in stews or dried and pounded for meal and pemmican. The taste of the summer berries may be strange to some palates but the berries are not poisonous as so many have assumed.

BULRUSH, *Scirpus* (several species)

Description: Tall plants; stems are triangular in some species, round in others; found along streams and marshes. A cluster of seeds is found just below the tip. The plant often grows taller than a man. (Figure 50.)

Uses: The rootstalks are edible and should either be peeled and boiled or eaten raw. The center core of the root is especially tasty. The young shoots just protruding from the mud are a delicacy raw or cooked, preferably raw. (Figure 51.) They are harvested by wading into the water and feeling down along the last shoot in a string of shoots that protrudes above the water. The hands are pushed into the mud until the lateral rootstalk is found. By feeling along the rootstalk away from the last shoot there is often found a protruding bulb from which the new shoot is starting. This is easily snapped off and is edible on the spot. When the only available water is brackish and unfit to drink, these young shoots will allay thirst for a long time.

The rootstalks when peeled, dried and pounded into flour make a good bread. This flour can be mixed with a flour made from the seeds of the

Fig. 49. Bracken Fern.

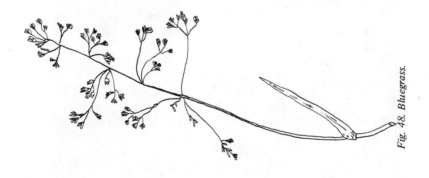

Fig. 48. Bluegrass.

52

Fig. 50. Bulrush.

Fig. 51. Bulrush shoots cooked by steaming under a pile of grass in the fire pit.

same plant. These are harvested by stripping and winnowing and are an important source of grain food.

The slender stalks are generally too tough for eating, but they are useful as a material for cordage, sandals, baskets and mats. (See "Weaving," p. 168.)

BURDOCK, *Arctium lappa, Arctium minus*

Description: Every farmer knows this bothersome weed. It is characterized by its large rhubarb-like leaves and purple flowers that produce a soft bur. The leaves are often over ten inches wide and a foot long. They are smooth and velvety to the touch. The burs are characterized by a mass of slender hooked spines that are not stiff. They cling to clothes and socks but seldom prick the skin. (Figure 52.)

Fig. 52. Burdock.

Uses: This useful plant has long been used in medicine for various external and internal complaints but generally as a tonic. The young leaves and shoots are edible cooked as greens. The root of the first year plant is an excellent food when fried or roasted.

The young stalks of the burdock can be peeled of its tough, bitter rind and the pithy center boiled for food. The roots can be dried and stored.

Fig. 54. Camas with large bulb.

Fig. 53. Camas in bloom.

Fig. 55. Some tough boys washing and preparing camas bulbs.

Fig. 56. Cattail.

BURREED, *Sparganium*

Description: This plant looks like the common cattail but lacks the long terminal spike and brown seed head. The seed head of the burreed is round, resembling a bur, and is mostly found along the side of the stalks. The leaf blades are narrow and sometimes triangular in cross section.

Uses: The bulbous stem bases and tuberous roots of this plant are used for food much the same as cattails and bulrushes.

CAMAS, Quamash, *Camassia quamash*

Description: A member of the lily family growing in damp meadows, this plant is characterized by slender leaves radiating from the base that appear grasslike. The stem is usually tall (one to two feet) and topped with a spike of blue flowers. It should never be confused with the similar looking plant of the death camas, *Zigadenus,* which is only distinguishable to most people by having smaller yellow flowers. This mistake has often caused the death of wild plant eaters since the death camas is extremely poisonous.

Camas should only be harvested when the plant is in bloom to distinguish it from the white or death camas. It can be harvested at other times of the year by those who are very familiar with the plant's minute characteristics. It is possible after much observation of both kinds to distinguish between them before and after flowering. A few general characteristics of camas are: It is never found growing in dry rocky ground as is the death camas; the flowers are blue or milky colored, whereas the death camas has only smaller yellow flowers; the leaf blades of most death camas are slightly narrower than most species of camas; generally the bulbs of large mature camas are much larger than the largest of the death camas. Camas grows mostly in the northern areas of the West—Idaho, Oregon and Washington. (Figures 53 and 54.)

Uses: The starchy bulb is an excellent food and can be gathered in large quantities with a digging stick. In meadows where these plants grow it is a simple matter to gather a bushel in just a few hours. The bulbs are best prepared by baking in a pit oven. After cooking they can be mashed and dried in cakes for storage. Camas bulbs were an important source of food to many of the early Indian tribes. (Figure 55.)

CATTAIL, *Typha latifolia, Typha angustifolia*

Description: Plants are found along streams and marshes throughout the West. It has long blade-like leaves sometimes six feet long and a jointless stem terminating in a sausage-shaped seed head. (Figure 56.)

Uses: The cattail is truly an outstanding plant. The roots, young shoots, seed heads and pollen are all edible, and the leaves make an excellent material for weaving. The fuzz from the head makes a good insulation for blankets and sleeping bags.

The roots when peeled and dried can be made into flour for bread. The starch can also be obtained from the root by soaking the mashed roots in water and stirring it vigorously. After the stirring process it should be allowed to sit overnight or until all the starch settles to the bottom of the container. The water is then poured off and the starch used as dough can be mixed with coarser seed flour for bread making.

The young shoots are excellent eaten raw or boiled like asparagus. The centers of the older shoots can be eaten in the same way but are not as good.

In the early summer the spikes at the top of the seed head form clusters of pollen which is yellow colored and very light and fine. It may be stripped from the stalks with the fingers and put in tight containers or bags to be used as flour for bread. It is especially good mixed with coarser grain flour.

The green head, before the pollen appears, is boiled and eaten like corn-on-the-cob. When dry, the heads are burned, leaving only the tiny roasted seeds which can be eaten as mush or ground for flour. It takes a large amount of cattail heads to yield a small amount of seed.

The down stuffed between two blankets that have been sewn together will give excellent insulation in cold weather; stuffed into shoes it will help prevent frostbite. The leaves, stripped and dried, can be used to make matting and other woven materials like sandals, baskets, blankets and ponchos. (See "Weaving," p. 168.)

CEDAR, Juniper, *Juniperus*

Description: Evergreen shrub or tree with blue berries in place of cones. This tree is very common in the foothills and desert portions of the West. (Figure 57.)

Uses: The small blue berries of the juniper can be eaten in an emergency. They are bitter tasting but nutritious. By pounding and boiling them, some of the resinous taste is removed. The inner white bark, stripped and pounded into a meal, will stave off starvation for a time.

The wood of the juniper is an easily obtainable bow wood and was much used by the early Indians. It is necessary to back juniper wood bows with sinew for long-lasting results.

CHICORY, *Cichorium intybus*

Description: This plant resembles the leaves of a dandelion except that the stem is branching and stiff. In late summer blue flowers appear on the stiff irregular stalks.

Fig. 57. Juniper berries.

Uses: The leaves are used for a potherb much the same as dandelions. The roots are edible in emergency situations.

CHOKECHERRY, *Prunus*

Description: This tree or shrub is easily recognized in the fall by its clusters of red-black cherries. The bark is reddish-grey and somewhat specked with lateral lines that resemble the domestic cherry tree.

Uses: The cherries of this tree are an excellent food despite the cyanogenetic poison contained in the seed. Slightly dried and crushed, seeds and all, on a mortar and dried in cakes, these berries provide nourishment that is lasting and satisfying. The dried cakes should be cooked before eating to help drive off the poison from the seeds. Pemmican is made by mixing fat and pounded dried meat with the meal of chokecherries and sealing it in gut or moulding it into round balls for preservation.

COTTONWOOD, Aspen, Poplar, *Populus*

Description: Large trees along streams at most elevations. They have rough grey bark and flowers in drooping catkins, borne in broad disks. The buds are resinous. The leaves are serrate and long-petioled.

Uses: The buds and leaves often provide a honeydew made by aphids that is edible. It is scraped from the leaves or boiled and skimmed off the surface of the water. The bark and sap of the tree are useful emergency foods.

CURRANT, *Ribes* (several species)

Description: Shrub three to ten feet tall with toothed leaves and berries forming in clusters. The berries are either golden, red or black.

Uses: The berries ripen early and provide excellent food to be eaten fresh or dried. They may be prepared in any of the ways mentioned for chokecherries. They contain no poisonous principles and can be used in large amounts.

ELDER, Elderberry, *Sambucus*

Description: This large shrub is characterized by a large, pithy, brown-colored stem with opposite compound leaves. The berries hang in globular clusters and are deep purple when ripe.

Uses: The ripe berries in the fall are an important food. They can be eaten raw or cooked. They keep dried and often lose their rank flavor, making them better tasting. The flower clusters may be eaten dipped in a batter and fried or crushed into stew. The green leaves and stems of the plant are said to be poisonous.

EVENING PRIMROSE, *Oenothera*

Description: Low plants with large white flowers or may be represented by species growing taller with yellow flowers. The plant is coarse with long leaves growing from the crown of the root in the low-growing species. The taller plant of yellow evening primrose is rather stiff and erect. It may appear to be prickly and coarse. The flowers of all the species remain open during the night. (Figure 58.)

Uses: The seeds of various species can be eaten parched or ground into meal. Many of the species have bitter roots that are not very palatable. Some lose this property when cooked, but when made palatable, the roots are an important source of food in the foothill and mountain areas.

FALSE DRAGONHEAD, *Dracocephalym* (mint family)

Description: Square stemmed plant of the mint family with a tufted seed head at the top of the stem. The leaves are simple and lanceolate in shape and opposite.

Fig. 58. Evening Primrose.

Uses: The seeds of this plant are edible ground on a metate for bread or cooked for mush.

FESCUE GRASS, *Festuca*

Description: Grass common to dry plains and desert foothills; slender erect stems with few basal leaves; long seed spikes.

Uses: The seeds are parched to remove the husk and used for mush or ground into flour.

FIDDLENECK, *Amsinckia tessellata*

Description: Plant with bristly hairs covering the entire plant. It is slender with the leaves alternate; seed head simple with the seeds in the form of small nutlets.

Uses: The nutlet seeds are gathered and used for food. Ground on a metate they make a good meal for mixing with other flour for bread cakes.

FISHHOOK CACTUS, *Echinocactus* and other species of *Cactaceae*

Description: Cactus with spines sometimes hooked or curved.

Uses: Seeds edible. When cooked the flesh is palatable.

FOXTAIL GRASS, *Chaetochloa*

Description: Grass with dense "fox-tail" seed spikes with long, stiff bristles. It is a common species of wasteland and desert seeps.

Uses: The grain of this plant is similar to wheat and is easily obtained by parching to remove the husk. The seeds ground for flour or boiled for mush provide excellent nourishment.

GOLDENROD, *Solidago*

Description: Tall plant with a large head crowded in a cluster. The leaves are often toothed and hairy, being alternate on the stem.

Uses: The seeds are gathered for food and used for mush and thickening for stew.

GROUND CHERRY, Husk Tomato, *Physalis*

Description: Low trailing vine with yellow flowers that later form into balloon-like husks or bladders. Inside the bladders are contained small tomato-like fruits. The leaves are usually oblong or ovate and bluntly pointed. (Figure 59.)

Uses: The fruit makes a good ingredient for stew and may also be eaten raw. They can even be baked in dough for small "pies."

HAIRGRASS, *Deschampsia*

Description: Fine grass of higher altitudes with narrow, firm leaf blades; spikelets sometimes purple and white. It is found in wet or damp soils.

Uses: Seeds may be harvested with seed beater and ground for mush and flour.

Fig. 59. Ground Cherry.

HAWKS BEARD, *Crepis*

Description: Plants usually found in moist or wet saline meadows. The leaves are mostly basal, lance-shaped and dissected into narrow divisions. The entire plant is covered with tiny hairs that impart a grey color sheen. The flowers are yellow. It has milky sap, and the seeds have silky white hairs at the top.

Uses: The young leaves are edible as a potherb and are often used to line cooking pits and then eaten with other foods prepared in the same pit.

HORSETAIL, Scouring Rush, Joint Grass, Snake Grass, *Equisetum fluvialile*

Description: The stems of this plant are of two kinds. One is sterile and many branched while the other is fertile and unbranched. This is the common joint grass so eagerly sought after by children for playthings. The grass is jointed and pulls apart easily. The top of the fertile plant has a brown head.

Uses: The young shoots in the spring can be used as a potherb during emergencies. Later the shoots become too stiff and contain a silica that gives them the name "scouring rush." It can be used for cleaning metal and for polishing and honing bone implements and wooden shafts. Pocketknives can be sharpened on this plant.

INDIAN POTATO, *Oroginia linariafolia*

Description: A tiny plant with basal leaves divided into slender leaflets looking like bird tracks. The stem arises from a deep nut-like bulb. (Figure 60.)

Fig. 60. Indian Potato.

Uses: This favorite bulb was much used by the Indians for food. They may be boiled, steamed, roasted or baked in any of the ways used to prepare potatoes. The tiny bulbs are tasty raw. They may be cooked and mashed into cakes for drying and keep indefinitely when protected from moisture. The hard cakes may be soaked and cooked in stew or soup. This is one of the tastiest roots found in the West. It grows in meadows and on mountainsides at higher altitudes. (Figure 61.)

INDIAN RICEGRASS, *Oryzopsis hymenoides*

Description: Grass with slender stems and flat or inrolled leaves. The seed head is tufted and contains large grains. Found on sand dunes and desert areas.

Fig. 61. Preparing Indian potato roots for cooking.

Uses: Seeds eaten. This grain is abundant and easily harvested.

JERUSALEM ARTICHOKE, Sunflower, *Helianthus tuberosus*

Description: A species of sunflower introduced from the Midwest and found growing in waste areas. They are usually more slender plants than the native sunflower of the West. The roots have large potatolike roots in the fall.

Uses: The large tuber is edible and formed an important food for the Indians of the Midwest. It has mostly escaped cultivation in the West and is not generally found in unsettled areas.

LAMB'S QUARTER, Goosefoot, Pigweed, *Chenopodium album*

Description: Common weed of wastelands and stream banks. The leaves vary from ovate to lanceolate in the various species. The seeds form in clusters. (Figure 62.)

Uses: The leaves and stems are edible when young. They can be eaten as salad or cooked like spinach. The seeds are edible ground for bread.

MANNAGRASS, *Glyceria*

Description: Grass with long narrow leaves and long seed head. It is

Fig. 62. Harvesting Chenopodium *seeds.*

often found growing on stream banks and around seeps. The long leaves sometimes hang into the water and float.

Uses: The seeds are gathered with a seed beater and winnowed to remove the chaff. They may be used as a thickening for stews and soups or ground on a metate for flour. This is one of the better-tasting grains found growing in the West.

MAPLE, Box Elder, *Acer*

Description: Tree with three-lobed leaves and winged seeds; common to mountain valleys and gullies.

Uses: The winged seeds are roasted and eaten. The sap, obtained by drilling a hole in the tree and draining through a tube (in the early spring), is an excellent drink. The inner bark is an emergency food when pounded for flour.

Fig. 63. Milkweed.

MILKWEED, *Asclepias syriaca*

Description: Plant with stout stems bearing opposite, entire leaves with broad midribs. The broken stems and leaves emit a milky sap. The large pods formed after flowering bear seeds that are plumed with silky fibers. (Figure 63.)

Uses: If care is taken to distinguish between the deadly dogbane which is similar, the young shoots may be cooked and eaten. The sap is heated for chewing gum. The very young seed pods can be boiled and eaten also. The fibers of the stalk are used to make cordage and fish line.

MINER'S LETTUCE, Indian Lettuce, *Montia*

Description: A small succulent plant with round fleshy leaves, some of which are united on both sides (or nearly so) to form a rounded disk or cup. (Figure 64.)

Uses: This tasty plant is the rival of garden lettuce for salads and raw greens. It can be eaten in large quantities. When mixed with water cress and placed between two hot cakes made of Indian potato root dough, this plant is unexcelled for flavor. The combination is a rare and satisfyingly new type of sandwich easily made in the wilds.

Fig. 64. Miner's Lettuce.

Fig. 65. Mint.

MINT, *Mentha* and other members of the mint family

Description: Most members of this family are characterized by a square stem. The leaves are opposite and lanceolate. (Figure 65.)

Uses: Catnip, peppermint, horehound, spearmint, horsemint, sage, thyme, hyssop and several other plants of the mint family are used for food and drink. As drinks they are unmatched for their soothing qualities. Headache, nausea, colic and other nervous upsets occurring in the wilds can often be relieved by a relaxing drink of mint tea. The seeds can be eaten or added to the leaves for steeping.

MORMON TEA, Brigham Tea, Squaw Tea, *Ephedra*

Description: Shrub with stiff, green-colored branches that are jointed; no leaves. It is found in the southern portions of the West and is quite conspicuous. (Figure 66.)

Fig. 66. Mormon Tea.

Uses: The green stems are steeped for a soothing and effective drink.

MOUNTAIN DANDELION, False Dandelion, *Agoseris aurantiaca*

Description: Looks like the common dandelion with its yellow flower. The leaves are not toothed as in the common dandelion. (Figure 67.)

Uses: The leaves are edible when cooked. The hardened sap or juice from the root and stems are edible or used as chewing gum.

MOUNTAIN LOVER, Myrtle Boxleaf, *Pachistima myrsinites*

Description: This evergreen shrub-like plant is found growing in patches under groves of trees in the mountains. The upper halves of the opposite leaves are toothed. The flowers are formed in clusters at the leaf angles.

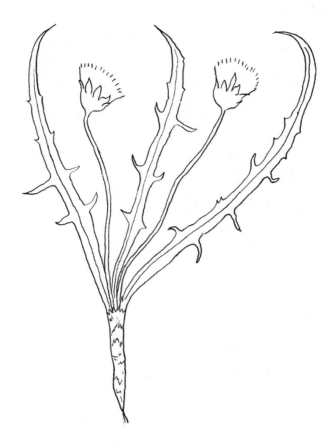

Fig. 67. Mountain Dandelion.

Uses: The berries are edible cooked in stew.

MULE'S EARS, *Wyethia amplexicaulis, Wyethia helianthoides*

Description: (1) *Wyethia amplexicaulis* has flower heads resembling the sunflower. They are bright or orange-yellow in color with several heads on a stalk. The plant itself is low to the ground and the leaves are erect and glossy. (2) *Wyethia helianthoides* is similar, having white flowers and a sticky, hairy stalk. The two species often cross-produce hybrids with yellow flowers and hairy stalks.

Uses: The seeds are edible and the roots of *Wyethia helianthoides* are eaten after long cooking.

MUSTARD, *Sisymbrium* (many species)

Description: The common mustard weed of every barnyard and wasteland is evident in several forms. Generally it is a leafy weed, erect with yellow or white flowers. The leaves are often deeply cleft. One species is the common tumbleweed.

Uses: The seeds of all the species are edible. The young greens are also eaten as a potherb. Tumbleweed greens can be eaten like salad.

NETTLE, Stinging Nettle, *Urtica*

Description: Erect plant with opposite toothed leaves that are rather egg-shaped. The stalks, stems and leaves are covered with fine stinging hairs that are well-known to most picnickers.

Uses: The leaves and young stems are edible as cooked greens. They are gathered with gloves or by using large mullein leaves *(Verbascum)* as pads for the hands. The stinging properties leave when the plant is cooked.

OAK, *Quercus*

Description: The common scrub oak of the mountains.

Uses: The acorn may serve as an emergency food but must be leached.

ONION, Wild Garlic, Nodding Onion, *Allium*

Description: Small plants resembling the domestic onions. They always have the familiar onion smell when the leaves are bruised. Plants looking like onions but lacking the smell should be checked closely as some species such as death camas, *Zigadenus,* are very poisonous. Late in the season these small onions may be found by finding the stalk supporting the dried flower head which looks like a white ball against the ground. (Figure 68.)

Uses: The whole plant is edible cooked or raw. Wild onions are excellent additions to any dish.

OREGON GRAPE, *Mahonia repens*

Description: These plants are holly-like shrubs growing low to the ground in dense thickets and under trees. The leaves are spined and dark green. (Figure 69.)

Uses: The deep purple berries are edible and quite tasty. They may be dried for future use.

Fig. 69. Oregon Grape.

Fig. 68. Wild Onions.

PINYON PINE, *Pinus monophylla, Pinus edulis*

Description: Evergreen pine tree growing in many areas of the West. It is characterized by its spreading growth and dense covering of pine cones containing large seeds. Most pine trees that bear cones do not have the large seeds.

Uses: The cones are gathered and charred in a fire to roast the seeds and loosen them. The seeds are then beaten from the cones and used as one of the most important foods available in nature. They may be eaten shelled or ground shell and all on a metate for a meal.

PLANTAIN, *Plantago major, Plantago lanceolata*

Description: These common lawn pests have either flat leaves, *Plantago major,* or long lanceolate shaped leaves, *Plantago lanceolata.* They are dark green and ribbed. The seed heads are in dense clusters at the end of long stems. The whole plant is only about eight inches tall. (Figure 70.)

Uses: The young leaves can be eaten. It is also an important herb for dressing wounds. (See "Mild Medicinal Plants," p. 91.)

PONDWEED, *Potamogeton*

Description: Underwater plant with string-like branches and leaves. They appear threadlike.

Uses: The rootstalks are edible cooked in stew.

PRICKLY LETTUCE, *Lactuca*

Description: This common weed is characterized by several species, most having narrow leaves that are lobed. The plant bleeds a milky juice when injured. (Figure 71.)

Uses: The young leaves are edible when cooked. The gum of the roots is made into chewing gum.

PRICKLY PEAR CACTUS, *Opuntia*

Description: Cactus with pear-shaped pads. They are found growing in patches. (Figure 72.)

Uses: The pads and fruit are edible raw or cooked.

PURSLANE, *Portulaca oleracea*

Description: Small fleshy weed growing low to the ground. The leaves are smooth and rounded on the ends. The stems are usually rose colored and juicy. (Figure 73.)

Fig. 71. Prickly Lettuce.

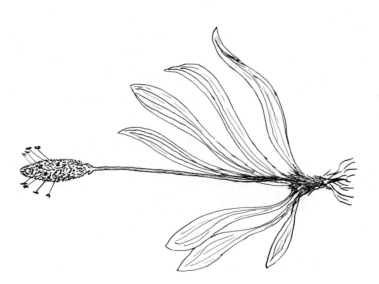

Fig. 70. Plantain.

Fig. 72. Prickly Pear Cactus.

Fig. 73. Purslane.

Uses: The whole plant is edible as a salad or as a potherb.

RABBITBRUSH, *Chrysothamnus*

Description: Stiff spiny brush growing in alkaline soils usually around water holes and lakes. The plant is light colored with light green "new stems" at the tops.

Uses: The new green tips of the brush are edible in the spring. The secretion at the top of the roots is chewed for gum.

RASPBERRY, *Rubus leucodermis*

Description: Common wild raspberry of higher elevations.

Uses: Berries are edible in season. They are not dried for future use.

RED CLOVER, *Trifolium pratense*

Description: Wild clover resembles the domestic variety with its round flower head and three leaves.

Uses: The seeds are edible as well as the greens. The steeped leaves are reputed to be good for colds and coughs.

REDTOP GRASS, *Agrostis*

Description: Grass with large seed heads covered with hairy bristles that have a reddish hue. It is a common hay grass.

Uses: The seeds are harvested with a seed beater and ground on a metate for flour or meal.

REED, *Phragmites communis*

Description: Very tall grass with stems resembling cane or bamboo. These plants are found in wet ground by streams and lakes. (Figure 74.)

Uses: The seeds are eaten as well as the rootstalks. The stems are used for arrows. (See "Arrow Making," p. 148.)

ROSE, Wild Rose, *Rosa*

Description: Every camper knows this thorny bush. The plant is similar to the domestic rose bush and usually has reddish-colored stems with bright red fruit maturing after the first frost in the fall. (Figure 75.)

Uses: The rose hips or berries are a ready supply of nutritious food

Fig. 74. Reeds.

Fig. 75. Rose Hips.

lasting through the fall and often all winter. They are easily picked and ground on a metate for a meal or flour. The fresh fruit is good cooked. The numerous seeds are hard and must be cracked or ground before eating. Rose hips contain a massive dose of vitamin C and are, therefore, valuable in cold weather.

SAGEBRUSH, *Artimisia biennis, Artimisia dracunculus*

Description: A green brush two to three feet high; common in dry desert areas.

Uses: Seeds may be eaten in emergency. They must be cooked. The bark has many uses for bags, rope, sandals, tinder, etc.

SALSIFY, Oysterplant, Goatsbeard, *Tragopogon*

Description: The leaves are grasslike and slightly hairy, giving them a queer translucent appearance around the edges. The second year plants produce yellow or blue flowers that later form large seed heads with umbrella-like fluffs that carry the seeds away in the wind. (Figures 76 and 77.)

Uses: The first year roots are edible cooked. The first year plant produces only leaves and is often hard to recognize. The root tastes like steamed oysters and is a rich food in the wilderness.

SAMPHIRE, *Salicornia*

Description: Small branching plant with fleshy stems reaching up clawlike. They are found in saline bogs and marshes. The fleshy plant is light green and looks like the fermented feet of chickens, if one can imagine that. (Figure 78.)

Uses: The plant is edible cooked and is a rich source of salt. Added to stew they provide all the salt flavoring necessary.

SEGO LILY, *Calochortus nuttallii*

Description: Small grass-like leaves showing among the brush and trees in the foothills. Later a stem appears bearing a lovely flower that is beyond description in its beauty. It is creamy white with light purple splotches at the base of the petals. It is the state flower of Utah and should only be harvested in emergencies or for scientific purposes. At one time the plant was thought to be in danger of extinction. Now it is very common, being quite thick in many areas. The fact that all the plants do not bloom makes it appear that they are rare. (Figure 79.)

Uses: The tender bulb dug with a digging stick is unsurpassed in flavor when roasted or boiled. The bulbs may be cooked and mashed into cakes for preservation.

78

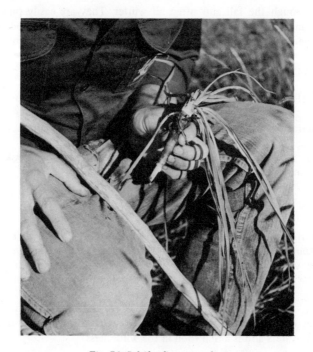

Fig. 76. Salsify, first year plant.

Fig. 77. Salsify, second year plants.

Fig. 78. Samphire.

*Fig. 79. Sego Lily in August. The plant matures early and
is represented in the dry form from July to March.*

SERVICE BERRY, *Amelanchier alnifolia*

Description: Tree bearing small apple-like fruit about the size of chokecherries. The fruit has tufted ends like the end of an apple. They are often confused with haws, *Orataegus.*

Uses: The berries are eaten raw or cooked. Mashed and dried in cakes they keep indefinitely. They can be mixed with pounded jerky for pemmican.

SHEPHERD'S PURSE, *Capsella bursa-pastoris*

Description: This plant is a common weed with toothed leaves and winged seeds. It is one of the earliest maturing mustards.

Uses: The seeds are edible cooked and ground for meal or mush.

SORRAL DOCK, *Rumex acetosella*

Description: This plant resembles the sour dock, *Rumex crispis,* except that it is smaller and the seed heads are red. (Figure 80.)

Uses: The young leaves are good cooked like dandelion greens.

SOUR DOCK, Curly Dock, Yellow Dock, Indian Tobacco, *Rumex crispus*

Description: The large lanceolate leaves are dark green and the dark brown seed clusters are conspicuously apparent in wastelands.

Uses: The young leaves are edible as potherbs. The seeds may be leached and used for an emergency food.

SPIKERUSH, *Eleocharis palustris*

Description: Green plant growing in marshes with long spike stems topped with a brown seed head. It has no leaves.

Uses: The seeds are edible and the stems are used in weaving.

SPRING BEAUTY, *Claytonia lanceolata*

Description: This tiny plant is found in wooded areas and has tiny white or pink flowers early in the spring. The leaves come in one pair and are opposite. The plant grows from a round nut-like corm. (Figure 81.)

Uses: This is an important source of food in the spring. The small bulbs are dug with a digging stick. They can be prepared any way that potatoes may be and will also preserve readily when cooked and mashed into cakes for drying.

Fig. 81. Spring Beauty.

Fig. 80. Sorral Dock.

STRAWBERRY, Wild Strawberry, *Fragaria americana*

Description: Exactly like the domestic variety only smaller.

Uses: The berry is eaten in season. The leaves steeped make an excellent hot drink.

SUMAC, Squawbush, *Rhus trilobata*

Description: Brush with three leaflets to a leaf with broad outer ends. The berries are in clusters and quite sticky. (Figure 82.)

Uses: The berries make an emergency food and an even better drink. The berries steeped in water and drunk cold are very refreshing.

Fig. 82. Sumac.

SUNFLOWER, *Helianthus*

Description: This is the common sunflower with which everyone is familiar. It has large yellow flowers and rather prickly stalks. (Figure 83.)

Fig. 83. Sunflower.

Uses: The seeds of sunflowers are perhaps the most nourishing food found in the wilds. Harvested with a seed beater and then ground on a metate, they are used as mush. They should not be cooked but just heated or eaten cold. These seeds provide an excellent baby food. The Indians depended on them to a great extent for that purpose.

THISTLE, *Cirsium*

Description: There are many species of thistles. Generally they may be described as succulent plants with many spines on the leaves and stems. (Figure 84.)
Uses: The young tender plant stems may be peeled and eaten. The roots are good when boiled with other food.

THORNAPPLE, Haw, Hawthorn, *Crataegus*

Description: These trees are the only native trees with thorns of any size. They look somewhat like an appletree and the fruit resembles miniature apples. (Figure 85.)
Uses: These berries are good food when dried and made into cakes. The dried cakes ground and mixed with pounded jerky make pemmican.

Fig. 84. Thistle.

Fig. 85. Thornapple in bloom.

UMBRELLA PLANT, Wild Buckwheat, *Eriogonum*

Description: Leafless stalks topped by compound umbles of tiny yellow or cream colored flowers. The stem arises from a dense cluster of leaves which are matted on the ground. The leaves are usually lance-shaped and are white on the bottom side. They occur in open areas of dry soil up to 9,000 feet.

Uses: The leaves are cooked for greens, and the seeds are edible when ground for meal or bread.

VIOLET, DOGTOOTH, Glacier Lily, *Erythronium grandiflorum*

Description: Lily with yellow flower and two large shiny oblong leaves arising from the base. The petals are very recurved. The bulb is deep and rounded. They are found growing at higher altitudes along streams and in shaded woodlands. (Figure 86.)

Uses: The root is dug with a digging stick but is difficult to obtain because it grows so deep. When obtained, the roots are excellent cooked like potatoes. The bulbs may be cooked and mashed for storage, and the leaves are also edible as greens.

WATER BUTTERCUP, *Ranunculus aquatilus*

Description: Plant growing in water with a white buttercup flower protruding above the water. The leaves are finely dissected into threads. They often grow in dense patches.

Uses: Most buttercups are poisonous, but this species is edible. The entire plant may be used as a potherb.

WATERCRESS, *Nasturtium officinale*

Description: Green leafy plant growing in clear water. The roots are white threads forming thick mats along the edges of streams. The leaves have three to nine segments. The tiny flowers are white.

Uses: Watercress is a favorite salad plant which has a delicate stingy taste which is most pleasant. It is used raw as greens. Watercress and miner's lettuce, *Montia,* wrapped together in tortillas made from root flour constitute an excellent wilderness sandwich.

WATER GRASS, Cockspur, *Echinochloa*

Description: Coarse annual grass with large leaf blades commonly found in waste ground and around deserted farms.

Uses: The seeds are harvested with a seed beater and ground for mush or flour.

86

Fig. 86. Dogtooth Violet.

WATERLEAF, *Hydrophyllum capitatum*

Description: This delicate plant is found growing at higher altitudes among dense growth of brush and trees on damp hillsides. The flower is a globular head of white to purple flowers which are tiny. The leaves are broad, fleshy and deeply divided with rounded tips. (Figure 87.)

Uses: The whole plant is edible. The rootstalks are several tiny brown carrot-like appendages radiating from the base of the stem. They make excellent stew with the plant tops serving as the greens.

Fig. 87. Waterleaf.

WATER PLANTAIN, *Alisma*

Description: Plants are found growing in water with narrow leaves which are ribbed and long. The fruit is in a compressed head.

Uses: The bulb is edible cooked and then dried. This process rids it of acrid properties.

WHEAT GRASS, Blue Joint Grass, *Agropyron*

Description: This is the common quackgrass and other similar species that are found throughout the West. The plant has a wheatlike seed head that contains a nutritious grain. (Figure 88.)

Uses: The seeds are harvested with a seed beater and ground on a metate. This seed can be harvested in goodly amounts with a little patience.

88

Fig. 88. Wheat Grass.

WILD HYACINTH, *Brodiaea*

Description: A plant easily confused with camas, *Camassia quamash,* and wild onions, *Allium.* The flowers are blue and form a cluster or umbel at the top of a slender stalk with two narrow basal leaves. The bulb is somewhat flattened on the bottom. (Figure 89.)

Uses: The bulb is an important food source in higher elevations. It is best cooked and eaten with greens or mashed and dried for future use in stews. Digging it with a digging stick is difficult since the bulb is deep.

WILD RYE, *Elymus*

Description: Common bunch grass seen along roadsides and in deserts. It is tall and coarse and the leaves are flat. There is a single erect spike of

Fig. 89. Wild Hyacinth.

seeds at the end of each stem.

Uses: The seeds harvested by stripping or with a seed beater and carefully winnowed make an excellent grain for mush and flour.

YAMPA, *Perideridia gairdneri* or *Carum gairdneri*

Description: This slender plant grows on damp hillsides and meadows in the foothills of the plateau area. The leaves are compound with narrow grass-like leaflets. The leaves usually dry up by flowering time. The flowers are in small white compound umbels. This plant is a member of the parsley family and positive identification is necessary.

Uses: The small finger-like roots grow deep and are sometimes in groups of two or three. They are perhaps one of the most important as well as most tasty roots found. They far outrank potatoes in flavor, and may be cooked in any of the ways that potatoes are prepared. When cooked and mashed into cakes for drying, they will keep indefinitely.

YELLOW FRITILLARY, Yellowbell, *Fritillaria pudica*

Description: Small plant with a single yellow or golden flower on a bent stalk so that it hangs either sideways or down. The leaves are lanceolate and basal. It is a pretty little flower found among the brush on damp hillsides. The root is a corm with a cluster of tiny rice-like bulblets surrounding it.

Uses: The corm is edible as well as the rice-like bulblets. When cooked, they resemble rice in looks and taste. The green seed heads are also edible when cooked.

Mild Medicinal Plants

BURDOCK, *Arctium lappa*

The young roots of the first year plant dug in the early spring or late fall are often used as a salve or wash for burns, wounds and skin irritations.

CATTAIL, *Typha,* Cattail Family

Use the white starchy roots pounded and mixed with animal fat for a salve in dressing burns.

CHOKECHERRY, *Prunus*

Inner bark is sometimes used as a tea to check diarrhea.

CURLY DOCK, Sour Dock, *Rumex crispus*

Roots are mashed and used for a poultice on sores and swellings.

CYMOPTERUS, *Cymopterus*

Old roots are said to be an effective insecticide when boiled.

MULLEIN, *Verbascum* (Figure 90.)

Burned leaves as an incense are said to be useful in lung congestion.

NETTLE, Stinging Nettle, *Urtica*

The root and leaves are said to be good for stopping diarrhea.

PEPPERMINT, *Mentha*

This plant is an aromatic stimulant and will often relieve nausea, colic, nervous headache and heartburn.

PINES, *Pinus,* Pine Family

1. The pitch of the lodgepole pine is useful for disinfecting and protecting open sores.
2. The Western White Pine is useful in coughs and upset stomach. Boil young shoots and use as a mild drink or cough syrup.

PLANTAIN, *Plantago lanceolate, P. Major*

The fresh leaves are a mild astringent and useful for cuts and wounds

Fig. 90. Mullein.

when mashed to a pulp and applied. They are also highly recommended to give quick relief for the external rectal irritation of piles.

SERVICEBERRY, *Amelanchier*

Boiled green inner bark is used for an eyewash.

SWEET FLAG, *Acorus calamus*

The root is said to relieve upset stomach.

WILD ONIONS, *Allium*

Rub the smashed leaves on arms and neck for an effective insect repellent. (Be sure to stay away from people because it is a people repellent also.)

WILD ROSE, *Rosa*

Very rich in vitamins A and C. Use berries as a tea or eat without cooking.

Fig. 91. Yarrow.

YARROW, *Achillea millefolium,* (Figure 91.)

1. The leaves are supposed to be good in stopping bleeding of wounds and reducing inflamation and healing rashes.
2. Chew leaves to relieve toothache.

Directions for Gathering Botanicals

1. Leaves should always be collected in clear dry weather in the morning after the dew is off. They are at their best when the plant is in bloom. Leaves of biennials are most valuable during the second year of their growth.
2. Flowers are worth more medicinally immediately upon opening.
3. Bulbs and roots should be gathered at the time the leaves of the plant die in the autumn for the best results.
4. Use only inner bark gathered preferably in the fall.

VI

ANIMAL LIFE AS FOOD

Animal life in the wilderness provides a substantial source of food. The taking of these lives for that purpose and for other needs such as clothing and tools requires a great deal of prowess and patience. Training to be a good hunter and trapper is necessary, but certain conditions should be observed during that training. All life, whether it is a tiny insect or a hot-tempered moose, has a sacred right to fulfill the measure of its creation. In no way can it be imagined that those fulfillments include making sport for man. Hunting for your existence is a different proposition altogether and reflects a more serious and mature relationship with nature. Hunger is humbling and killing creates a void in the earth that is eased not by boasting of trophies but by sincere need.

Hunting an animal is a challenge! If a need for the animal is present, one can certainly enjoy that challenge. Need implies putting the animal to *good* use. Every part of it may be used in a survival situation and it is inexcusable to waste even a shred.

The methods used to obtain game in a primitive situation are varied. Many of them are cruel and should be avoided unless no other way presents itself.

Insects

Some insects provide greater nourishment than any other animal source. Grubs and other immature insects are excellent sources and should never be neglected when foraging. When mashed and added to soups or stews, they are never distasteful. Ants are good for food in an emergency when harvested by scooping up a den with a winnowing tray and pouring on a heap of hot coals to kill and roast them. It is a rather picky job to get them properly winnowed away from the coals. The bodies when ground into a powder serve as a kind of black sugar.

Grasshoppers and helgramites, as well as a number of similar insects, are easily gathered and made palatable. They must be well cooked in order to kill parasites.

Small Rodents, Reptiles, Amphibians and Birds

Nearly every species of these small animals is palatable when prepared properly. They may be captured with deadfalls and snares set in places where they frequent. When setting traps it should be remembered that a lot of them will ensure a larger take. Traplines should be well planned and checked every day. A good line for small rodents would be a series of about twenty deadfalls strung along a cliff base in crevices and caves. Rats and mice are easily caught in these places, and twenty well-placed deadfalls will usually net from eight to twelve of them each night. Traps may be baited with roasted roots or cooked meat. (Figures 92, 93, 94, 95, 96, 97, 98, 99, 100, 101, 102, 103 and 104.)

Mice and other small rodents should be skinned, eviscerated and pounded to a pulp. When all the bones are pulverized, they are ready for the stew pot or to be added to a cooking pit full of tasty roots. The heads should be included in this little operation.

Reptiles and amphibians can be caught by hand and may provide a substantial meal on occasion. All reptiles and amphibians must be skinned before cooking. Frogs, lizards and snakes can be skinned and roasted or boiled and the entire body consumed. When killing rattlesnakes for food, care should be taken that the snake has no opportunity to bite itself, especially if the person cleaning it has an open cut or scratch on his hands. (Figures 105 and 106.)

Small birds should be considered as an emergency food only. They are rarely worth the effort to obtain unless they occur in large flocks. Various traps can be made to catch them. A throwing stick or bolas often work. These useful weapons are perhaps the easiest to construct and may serve admirably for a person who is adept at throwing.

The throwing stick is simply a hefty stick that has been worked down to a crude bevel, acting somewhat like a non-returnable boomerang. It skims along the ground for great distances and will stop any small to medium-sized game. A digging stick will serve as a throwing stick also.

A bolas is a series of stones (usually three) attached by means of straps or strings. They can be hurled at flying flocks of birds and larger game. Ducks are often easily caught this way. (Figure 107.)

Trapping Larger Game

Animals such as deer, bear, coyotes and bobcats may be taken in larger deadfalls. Bush and trail snares can be used on deer if they are set so that a person can detect immediately when one is caught and quickly kill it before it has a chance to tear loose. Night snares close to camp and daytime snares on trails where drives can be made are the most effective. *It must be noted that the taking of any game animal with traps is forbidden except during an extreme emergency when one is lost in the wilderness.*

Fig. 92. This simple "Figure 4" trail deadfall is used on game trails where the brush is thick enough to make the set inconspicuous. A V-shaped row of stakes fanning away from each approach to the trap will cause the game to go through rather than around the logs. It also is an excellent trap to set at the entrance to burrows and dens.

97

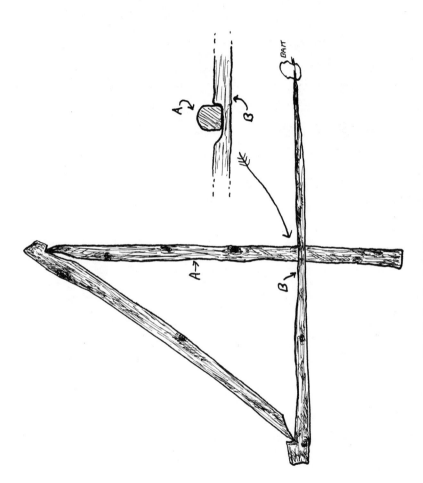

Fig. 93. Details of the "Figure 4" trap trigger.

Fig. 95. Ground squirrel caught in a "Figure 4" deadfall. Note that the trigger sticks did not flip out from under the rock as it fell. This indicates a poor set. The force of the release should have thrown the entire apparatus clear of the falling stone.

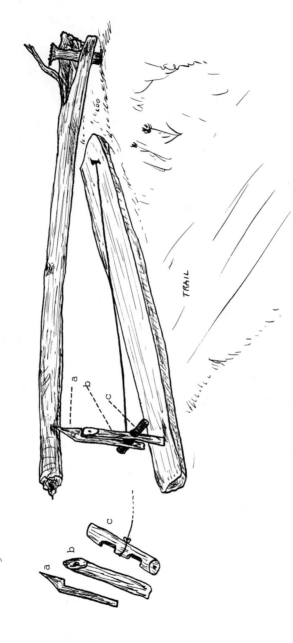

Fig. 96. Modification of the "Figure 4" trap trigger. The string is anchored across the path so that when the animal touches it the catch stick (c) is pulled from the offset support sticks (a and b). The kill pole is split at the bottom end and a stake is driven between to keep the pole from rolling off the support stick. Support stakes may also be driven on each side of the pole to ensure a straight drop.

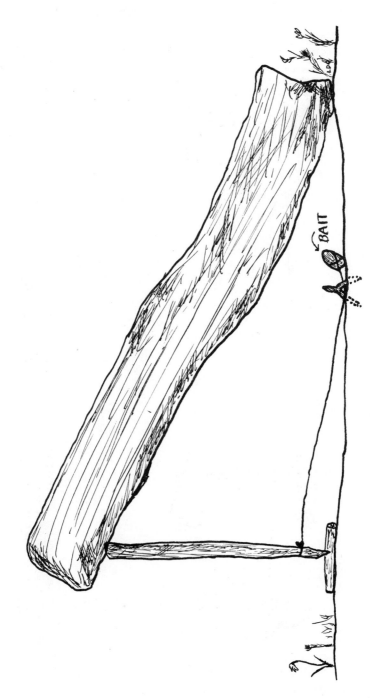

Fig. 97. Simple two-stick deadfalls supporting flat stones. These sets were commonly used by the Indians of the Great Basin to catch small game. They are simple to construct but are not as effective as the "Figure 4" type.

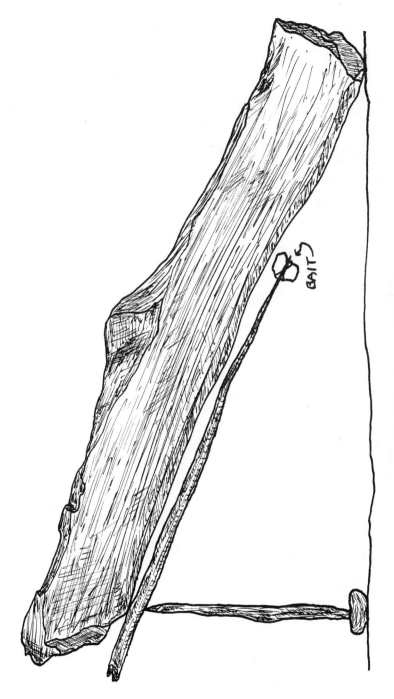

Fig. 98. Another two-stick deadfall.

102

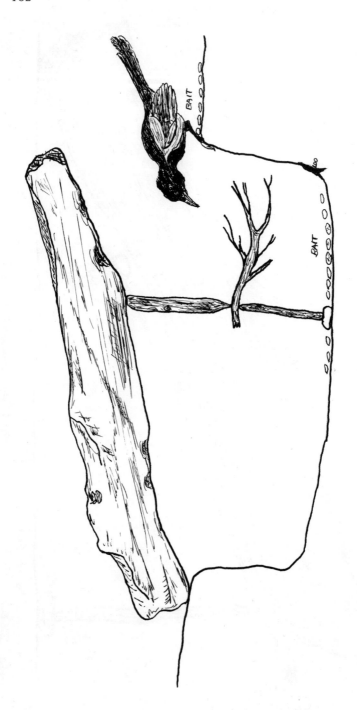

Fig. 99. Bird trap set so that the bird entering the pit will hop first onto the twig, thus causing the stone to fall. It is wise to check what you have caught before reaching under the rock for the game. These traps are known to have rattlesnakes as their captives.

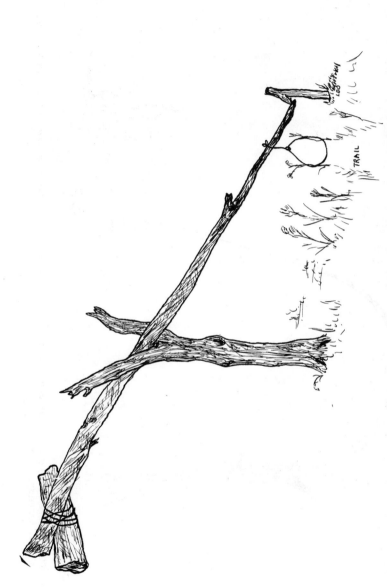

Fig. 100. Lift pole snare with a weight on the back end and that exceeds the weight of the animal to be caught. The animal coming down the trail is caught in the loop. Its struggles pull the tip of the lifting pole from its catch and the pole lifts it from the ground.

103

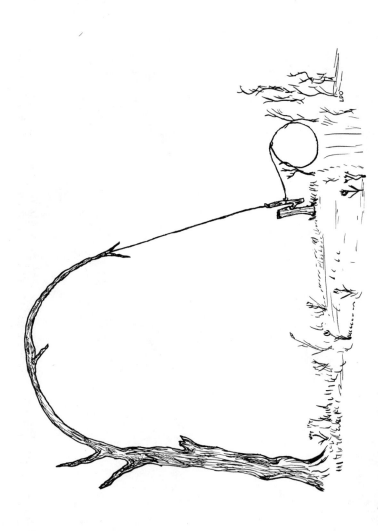

Fig. 101. Spring pole snare set on a trail. The animal does not need to be lifted entirely off the ground. As long as its front feet are in the air, it will not escape.

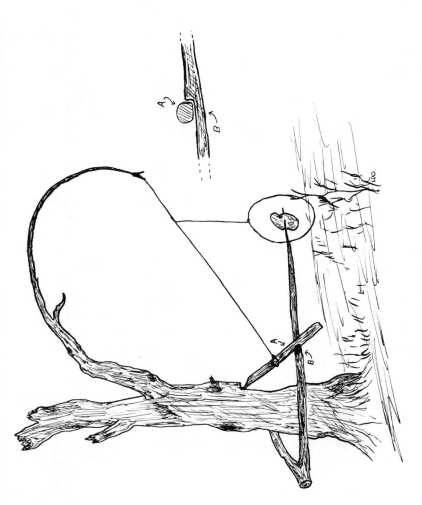

Fig. 102. Spring pole snare with baited trigger. The snare loop is placed where it will encircle the animal's neck as it reaches for the bait.

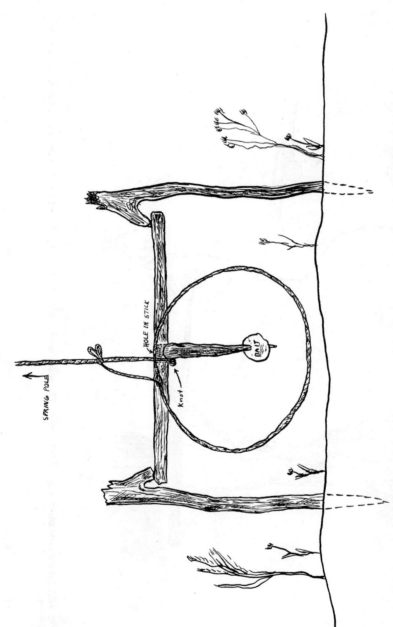

Fig. 103. Simple snare with bait. A hole is drilled in the cross stick and a string is threaded through with a knot in one end. The bait stick is lightly forced into the hole so the knot will not slip. A small fence is set up around one side of the set so that the animal must reach through the snare loop to get the bait.

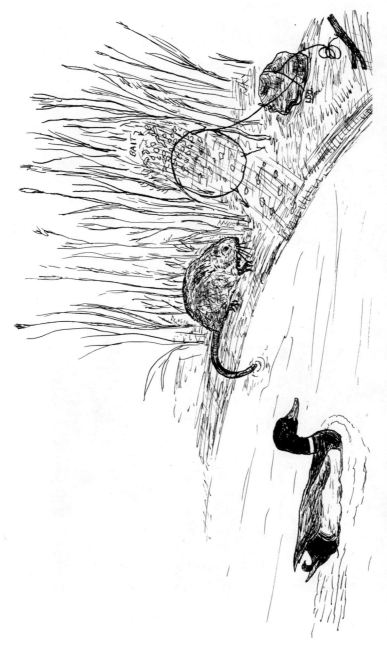

Fig. 104. Trail set snare placed in feeding run made by ducks and muskrats. The snared game drags the stone anchor into the water where it sinks, drowning its victim. It is a good idea to have a float tied with a string to the stone so the set can be found after it sinks.

Fig. 105. Rattlesnake-on-a-stick and carp smothered in ashes round out this meal.

Fig. 106. Outdoor survivalists try a tasty rattlesnake for dessert after a meal consisting of various roots, cattail shoots and fish.

Fig. 107. Bolas.

Hunting and Stalking

Obtaining game with primitive weapons is quite a different story from blasting away with a rifle at a deer running across the canyon from the hunter. It becomes necessary for a person to exercise all his ability to get close enough to his prey for his arrows or spear to be effective. (Figure 108.) Stalking deer and other large game is not difficult if the following steps are taken:

1. Of course, it is necessary for the hunter to spot the deer before it sees him.
2. He must keep down wind from the deer.
3. The deer's feeding habits should be watched until a pattern shows itself. Most deer will feed for about twenty seconds and then raise their heads for a look around. When its head is down the deer sees nothing but the grass it is eating.
4. When the animal has its head down, the hunter walks toward it slowly and counts to ten (ten seconds) and then stops. He must not press his luck by trying to gain a few more steps before the deer looks up. It may catch him in the middle of a step. No attempt should be made to hide. The hunter should stay relaxed because the wait may be a long one. After a few seconds the deer will raise its head and survey the country. It will see only movement and when it looks in the direction of

Fig. 108. Hunting with primitive equipment like this atlatl and spear requires much patience and stalking ability.

the hunter it may gaze at him for some time. If the hunter does not bat an eyelash, the deer will soon ignore him and continue feeding.

5. As soon as the deer drops its head again the hunter should walk forward for another ten steps and then freeze. This is kept up until the range is right for a good shot. Somehow a deer fails to comprehend that the old stump gets closer each time it looks at it.

Fig. 109. Calling game by smacking the lips against the back of the hand to produce the squeal of an aminal in trouble.

Deer can be ambushed at water holes during the early dawn hours or in the late evening. The secret to this is to be concealed in a spot that will not allow the deer to sense the hunter's presence and yet will allow a clear shot. Two or more people can drive deer past concealed hunters along well-used trails.

Many animals can be called to the hunter. The cry of a mouse or rabbit in pain will attract any carnivore as well as the animal imitated. There are a number of ways to make good animal calls but the simplest and perhaps the finest one involves only the lips and the back of the hand. A long, drawn-out kiss on the back of a wet hand will sound (with practice) like a squealing rabbit or mouse. Short smacks will give the call of a chipmunk or rockchuck. Indeed, with a little practice a number of calls can be developed using only the lips and hands. (Figure 109.)

Rockchucks and ground squirrels may be easily fooled by two hunters. An open approach is made to the animal's den, with one person whistling a

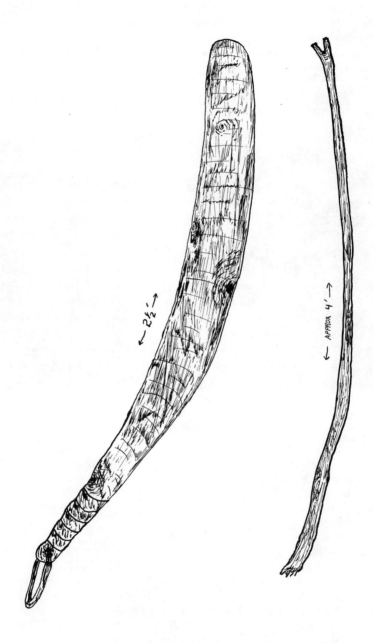

Fig. 110. Throwing stick and rodent skewer.

lively tune. When the animal dives for his hole the hunters just keep right on and the whistler, still whistling, walks on by and off into the distance. The other hunter quickly conceals himself in a position for a good shot and waits. The rockchuck, hearing the whistling fading in the distance will come out for a last look. If the concealed hunter is a good shot it *will* be a last look.

Sometimes a rodent can be dragged from its den with a rodent skewer. (Figure 110.) This simple device is made from a long supple willow with a fork in one end. It is thrust into the hole until the animal is felt. Then by gently twisting the stick, the forked end is caught in the animal's fur and wound tightly. By gently pulling and coaxing, the rodent is easily brought to the surface.

Ground squirrels and mice can be caught by flooding them from their holes. A diverted stream or buckets of water carried to the den will do the job. They can be killed with sticks as they emerge.

Fishing

Making fishing tackle that will catch fish requires some special skills in bone working and twisting fibers for line. The fibers best suited for line are stinging nettle *(Urtica)*, milkweed *(Asclepias)*, dogbane *(Apocynum cannabinum)*, and the bark of the haw tree *(crataegus)*. They are carefully selected and twisted tightly. (See "Cordage," p. 164.) About ten feet of line on a long willow pole will serve in most rivers and streams.

Fig. 111. Skewer hook made of bone.

Hooks are best made of bone. The simplest is the skewer hook. (Figure 111.) This is a sliver of bone that is tied at the middle and is turned parallel to the line and inserted into the bait. When the fish swallows the bait, the bone turns sideways and holds. Another simple device is the cross hook. The crosspiece is turned parallel to the main shank and the bait applied. When the fish swallows this, the cross piece is pulled sideways, thus, setting the hook. (Figure 112.)

Conventional hooks can be made of bone in the following manner:

1. A small thin-walled bone is selected and cut into a rectangle. Bird and rabbit bones are the only kinds thin enough.
2. The piece of bone is then drilled several times to remove the center portion. (Figure 113.)
3. Using a stone or bone punch, the partitions between the drill holes are worked out and the walls are smoothed with a small piece of sanding stone. This leaves a rectangular ring of bone.
4. The ring is cut in two places, leaving two hooks which are sharpened and attached to a lead line. (Figure 114.)

Hooks are attached to the line by a tight wrapping of fine string or fiber. The hook shank is first notched and then smeared with pitch or some other sticky substance. After the wrapping is attached, it is sealed with pitch. Hooks can be successfully tied on the line without the use of pitch if the wrapping is made tight in the notches.

Trout and other game fish in small streams are very hard to catch with these crude hooks and line. River fish such as carp, suckers, catfish, chubs, redhorse, squawfish and whitefish are easily caught and prove to be very tasty when fried or baked. (Figures 115 and 116.)

Fish Traps

A good fish trap will catch many more fish than a hook and line. There are a number of types. All are good. The type of trap to build depends on the nature of the stream or river. A person's ingenuity in using natural features to aid in making the traps will determine much of his success. (Figures 117, 118 and 119.)

Spearing Fish

Many fish feed in shallow water and are easily speared. The simplest spear is made from a willow about 14 feet long to which is bound a set of hardwood prongs. The prongs should be bound with more of the length attached to the shaft than what protrudes. This will ensure the sturdiness of the device when it gets rough use. Few fish will be lost if they are speared through the sides and then pinned to the bottom by quickly pushing the spear into an upright position and forcing it into the mud. (Figures 120, 121, 122, and 123.)

Detail of making hooks of bird bone.

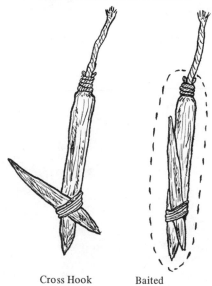

Cross Hook   Baited

Fig. 112. Details of hook making.

Fig. 113. Drilling bone for hooks.

Fig. 114. Two hooks made from a piece of bird bone.

117

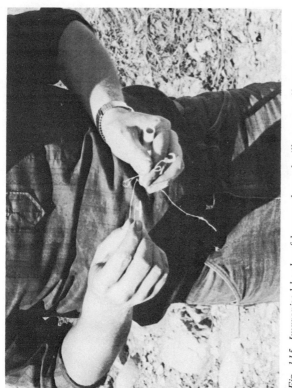

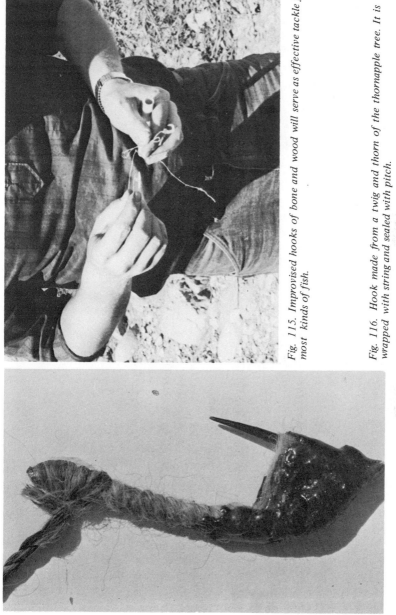

Fig. 115. Improvised hooks of bone and wood will serve as effective tackle for most kinds of fish.

Fig. 116. Hook made from a twig and thorn of the thornapple tree. It is wrapped with string and sealed with pitch.

118

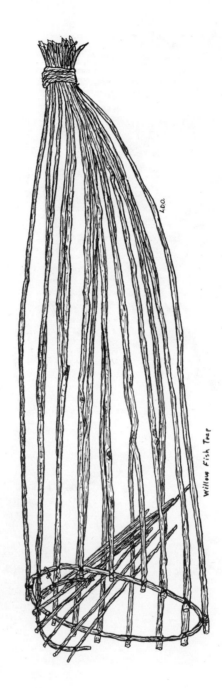

Willow Fish Trap

Fig. 117. Willow fish trap can be placed in streams in riffles between pools. A V-shaped barrier fence made of willows stuck in the mud leading to the opening will direct migrating fish into the trap.

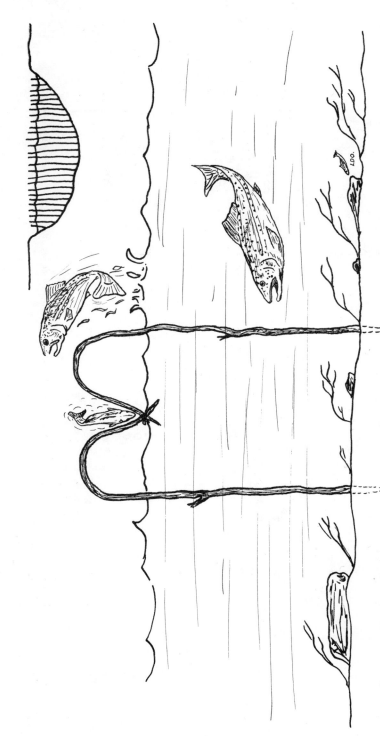

Fig. 118. Willows stuck in the mud to form two parallel rows about two feet apart and extending completely across the stream. The ends of the willows above the water are bent and tied together to form a trough about a foot deep. The fish trying to leap the barrier are caught and wedged in the trough.

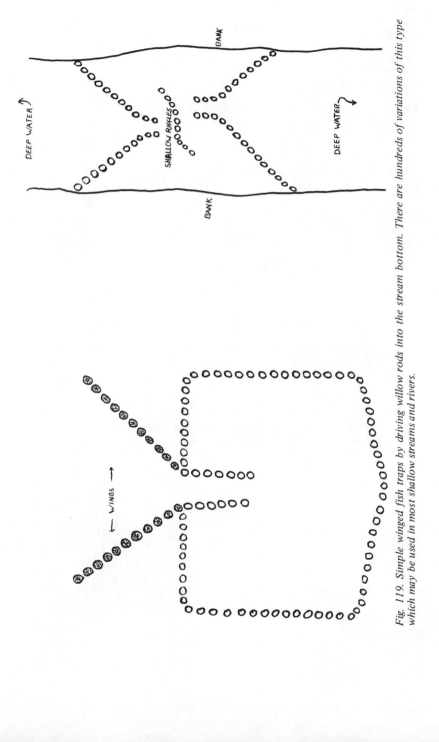

120

Fig. 119. Simple winged fish traps by driving willow rods into the stream bottom. There are hundreds of variations of this type which may be used in most shallow streams and rivers.

Fig. 120. Making a simple two-pronged fish spear.

Fig. 121. Wrapping the prongs on the shaft with twisted cattail leaves.

122

Fig. 122. Fishing with the spear.

Fig. 123. Speared fish.

There are a number of other types of spears that may be used. In a practical sense, none of them will serve any better than the simple one mentioned above. It may prove interesting to try them when the time warrants the effort to manufacture them. The illustrations show some of the more effective ones. (Figure 124.)

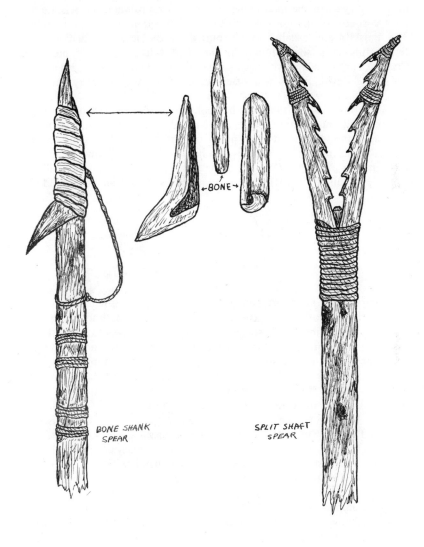

BONE

BONE SHANK
SPEAR

SPLIT SHAFT
SPEAR

Fig. 124. Fish Spears.

Other Types of Water Life

Most water abounds in all kinds of eatable life, and much of it is so easily caught that a person could live indefinitely from one small stream. Crayfish, mussels, helgramites, stoneflies, snails, tiny minnows and polliwogs are the most common. They are found by moving rocks and moss or digging in the mud along the shore. Crayfish and mussels are the most desirable of the lot and they can be gathered in fairly large amounts. The mussels are usually found buried in the mud. A shallow trail terminating in a slight hump in the mud will betray their presence. Crayfish appear in the evenings and can be caught by hand or with a hook and line. Moving rocks will often scare them out, but they must be grabbed quickly.

All forms of water life must be cooked immediately to avoid spoilage. Crayfish and mussels are traditionally cooked alive to avoid toxic spoilage. A more humane method is to pinch off the crayfish heads just before boiling or steaming. The mussels just have to be cooked alive by placing them in a steaming pit. (See "Cooking Pits," p. 39.) Mussels that will not close their shell up tight when touched may be sick or dead and should not be eaten.

Jerky, Pemmican and Dried Fish

Jerky

Meat will not keep very long in warm weather, so it is necessary to dry any surplus for future use. The standard "modern" methods of making jerky involve brines and spices which give the meat a rich flavor. However, these processes decrease the food value and render it so salty that a substantial meal of solely jerky would make a person quite sick.

Meat jerked for use as a food rather than a snack or delicacy must be prepared without brines and spices. It is simply cut into thin strips about ¼ inch thick and dried in the sun for a couple of days. When it becomes hard and brittle it is taken down and stored in a pit or in bags. It is used in stews and soups or just roasted lightly on the coals and eaten.

Cutting meat into strips may prove difficult when small chunks are involved. It is best to take a chunk and cut through it within ¼ inch of the other side. Then by turning the knife sideways it is cut or "unrolled" into a long strip. (Figure 125.)

Small animals and birds can be dried whole after skinning, eviscerating, cracking the back between the legs and inserting a stick to help hold the body cavity open. The animals are then laid on rocks in the sun to dry. When thoroughly dried, they are pounded to crush the bones. Another day in the sun will dry the marrow and ensure preservation. (Figure 126, 127, 128, 129 and 130.)

Fig. 125. Cutting or "unrolling" jerky.

Fig. 126. Drying jerky.

Fig. 127. Pounding jerky for eating.

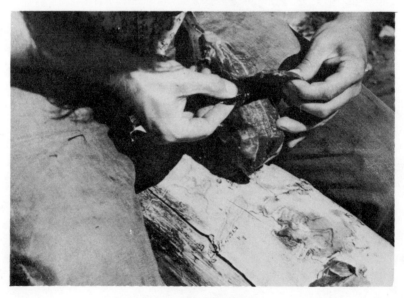

Fig. 128. Cutting meat into strips with a stone blade.

Fig. 129. Ground squirrel spread out to dry in the sun.

Fig. 130. Ground squirrel dried and ready for storage.

Pemmican

Pemmican is a mixture which surpasses the taste and nutrition of "K" rations. It is made by drying berries to take out the excess moisture and then pounding them into a paste. To this is added dried pounded jerky, and then melted suet is mixed with the berries and meat. The mixture is next rolled into small balls and stored in the cleaned intestines of a large animal. The intestine sack is tied shut, sealed with suet, and stored in a cool dry place. Pemmican prepared in this way will keep for several months. Balls of pemmican are also safely stored in plastic bags or leather bags richly soaked in melted suet.

Dried Fish

Small minnows are easily dried by spreading them out in the sun. Cleaning them is not necessary. Larger minnows over two and one-half inches should be eviscerated and split for drying. The sun will dry small fish in one or two days after which they may be kept in bags or in a storage pit. (See "Storage Pits," p. 43.)

Drying larger fish is accomplished in one of two ways. The simplest is to split the fish down the back and hang it on a rack for drying. This leaves the bones which make eating difficult. One way to get around the bothersome bones is to pound the dried fish into a fine meal to be used in stews. This crushes the larger bones and the finer ones are softened by cooking. A second method is to fillet the fish and dry the strips by hanging them on a rack in the sun. The meat is cut from the bones by splitting the fish down the back and removing the side strips by slicing along the ribs. There is some waste if the bones are not saved. In a survival situation waste is not tolerable, so it is important to use the remaining bones by slightly drying and grinding them into a meal for adding to stews.

All dried fish will keep a year or more if stored in a dry place. Eating dried fish is not a pleasant experience at first and there always remains the possibility of parasites. Therefore, it is best to cook it before eating. The advantage of pounding or grinding dried fish is to allow it to dry better, thus minimizing spoilage and reducing the space taken up by bulky chunks. The meal has many more uses than the whole strips. It can be used in bread, soup, stews, stuffings and mixed with cooked seed grains for a wholesome cereal. The meal can also be moistened, made into fish patties and fried.

SPECIAL SKILLS

Since a person living entirely off the land is restricted to using only the natural elements around him, it is imperative that he know how to use them effectively. This chapter will explain a few of the more important skills in making and using primitive tools. Common sense is the key to most skills and no doubt many methods will work for some of the things mentioned here.

The following skills are presented in the manner in which the author has personally used them while living off the land. They follow in this order: stone working, bone working, bow and arrow making, atlatl making and using, making cordage and weaving sandals and baskets, preparing sinew, rawhide and tanning.

Stone Working

Ancient man's survival depended in great measure upon his ability to utilize and modify his immediate surroundings. To accomplish the tasks of cutting, digging, scraping, chopping and building, he developed a remarkable array of tools made of stone. The skill required to produce workable tools of stone is a little more complex than one might imagine and shows a high degree of inventiveness and manual dexterity. Also the amount of work these tools can do is, indeed, remarkable.

A person thrown into a primitive survival situation would quickly find his existence greatly impaired without the aid of so simple a tool as a pocket knife. The question then arises: How can he survive without a knife to cut poles for building shelters and shafts for a spear or bow or to fashion the myriad of items essential to survive in nature? Nearly everything done requires the use of a cutting or chopping tool, either directly or indirectly by the use of other tools that were made with cutting and chopping tools. (Figure 131a.)

The following is an account of the more common primitive stone working methods that have been carefully researched and tested repeatedly by the author until mastery was achieved.

Lithic Arts

The processes of shaping stone can be divided into four major parts: (1) percussion flaking, (2) pressure flaking, (3) pecking or crumbling and (4) the abrading process. Other recognized processes such as incising and piercing are minor and can be included as simple variations of the abrading process under special conditions. They are used exclusively to shape very soft rocks such as soapstone.

130

Fig. 131. Cutting and chopping implements of stone.

Fig. 131a. Using a stone axe.

Percussion Flaking

Percussion flaking is a highly technical art, demanding precise skill and forethought. The process is divided into three methods: (1) direct percussion with a hammerstone, (2) indirect percussion with a hammerstone and a punch and (3) direct or indirect percussion with the stone resting on another larger stone (anvil). All three methods may be used in the production of a single piece of work.

Direct percussion, sometimes referred to as direct free-hand percussion, may be used to rough out large pieces of rock into usable blanks from which specialized tools may be fashioned or to shape blanks into serviceable specialized tools. In practice, the stone to be shaped is held in the left hand and fractured by blows from a hammerstone or horn baton held in the right hand. Simple axes and choppers can be made in this way from common ryolite or quartzite cobbles. The blows of the hammerstone should fall directly onto the edge of the core, especially if it is a rather thin one. This is necessary when working with chert, coarse agate, dull jasper or any other non-glassy stone. Holding the blank at an angle while striking off chips is often necessary to remove rough spots and trim the edges. Obsidian (the exception) and other similar glassy rocks cannot be chipped successfully by striking directly onto the edge of the core. It must be struck at an angle to avoid crumbling the edge and producing unwanted hinge fractures. (Figure 132.)

When blades for cutting or other specialized tools are wanted, it is necessary to produce a striking platform on the core. This is done by merely breaking a rock in half, leaving two cores, each with one flat surface. Striking blades from the core is then relatively easy. The secret to obtaining good blades from a core is to make sure the stroke carries all the way through. By working around the core with even strokes, a number of razor-sharp blades can be made before it is exhausted. (Figures 133 and 134.)

A blank with a difficult knob or thick edge in such a place as to make direct percussion impractical can be worked down indirectly with the aid of a punch made from deer horn or other horn of similar density. This requires the assistance of a second person. The blank is held in the left hand, which is protected with a leather pad, and the punch is placed against the edge and steadied with the other hand. The assistant then strikes the punch sharply with a hammerstone. In this way the force is applied to the exact spot intended.

Percussion flaking with the blank resting on another stone (anvil) works but is rarely necessary except in removing troublesome bulbs and for striking off larger flakes to thin down a thick blank. For this it is best to use the indirect percussion method while the blank rests on a padded anvil. (See Figure 132.)

132

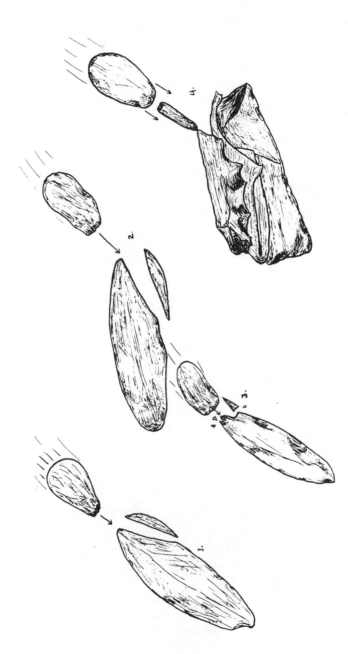

Fig. 132. (1) Striking directly into hard shale or cobble stone to remove flakes. (2) Striking at an angle with the hammerstone to remove flakes from glassy rock like obsidian or jasper. (3) The wrong way to remove flakes from glassy stones. (4) Removing flakes by indirect percussion.

Fig. 133. Striking blades from a core with a horn baton.

Fig. 134. Blade struck from core.

A variation of the indirect percussion method is to place the blank between the knees with the edge to be flaked facing up. The punch and hammerstone can then be used without the aid of an assistant. To prevent the chips from cutting the knees, the blank should be placed in the fold of a thick piece of leather. Variations of this sort are numerous among modern flint workers as was probably the case in aboriginal times. The differences in methods are a matter of preference. Basically, the simple use of the hammerstone or horn baton alone in shaping tools is the most practical form of percussion flaking.

Pressure Flaking

The more delicate job of finishing a blank into a specialized implement requires the simplest tools but a complex nervous system. A nervous Indian probably spent more time bandaging cuts than making arrowheads. A piece of horn and a leather pad are all that is needed to produce the

Fig. 135. Tools for pressure flaking stone.

finest knives and arrow points. (Figure 135.) A blank or blade produced by percussion flaking or even a simple chip of flint or obsidian is held in the palm of the left hand with the fingers gripping it firmly. The leather pad protects the hand from being cut. Then with the hand braced against the left knee small chips are pressed off with the horn flaker. The tip of the horn is placed on the edge of the flint and pressure is applied inward and downward against it. At the same time the horn is given a slight twist, causing the chip to come off on the underside of the blank. Considerable skill is required to do truly beautiful work, but serviceable tools can be made with a little practice. (Figures 136 and 137.)

A further consideration of the minute technicalities of pressure flaking shows that there is considerably more to it than the basics described above:

1. When the stone is gripped in one hand and braced against the knee, it must be held slightly forward on the heel of the hand so that the pressure from the fingers will tip the edge up. This allows the flaker tip to force the chip off the bottom side of the blank. Failure to do this may quickly reduce the number of fingers on even the most skilled Stone Age artisian.

2. The power of the wrist is not sufficient to flake larger pieces of stone. The force applied with the tip of the flaker must come from the weight of the body. The push should be fairly hard but not sudden. The best results are achieved by just leaning into it with a steady even pressure. Sudden hard lunges cause loss of control and often result in bad cuts.

3. The tip of the flaker is not sharpened to a fine point but is a blunt chisel shape. This allows it to grip the blank firmly.

4. The force is applied in the direction in which the flake should run. The idea is to make the flake run across the bottom face of the blank. If the tool is pushed downward at a 90° angle, the flake will be short and stubby.

5. The force of the flaker against the edge of the blank is accompanied by a slight twist. This makes the flake come off more readily. (Figure 138.)

The method of pressure flaking described above is the most widely used. A variation of it uses a stone anvil for the rest, much the same as is done by indirect rest percussion. The only difference is that the punch is used to press off the flakes instead of striking them off. Here again individual preference is the rule. At any rate, the varieties of methods used in percussion and pressure flaking can all be combined and modified to accomplish the task of flaking stone into useful tools.

The horn and leather are not indispensable to pressure flaking. It is only the student trained under civilized exactness that would not improvise suitable substitutes. As for the archaic craftsman caught out

136

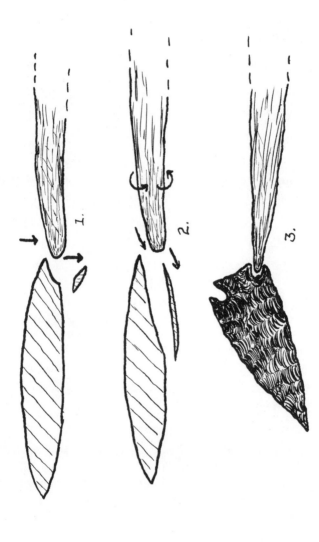

Fig. 136. Details of pressure flaking. (1) The wrong way produces short stubby flakes. (2) The right way. By pushing in the direction that the flake is to go and giving a slight twist with the flaker, a long thin flake will peel off the bottom side of the flake. (3) Notching is done with a fine-tipped flaker.

Fig. 137. Proper position for pressure flaking.

Fig. 138. Knife made from a fine-grained basalt. It was flaked by percussion. The arrow points are of agate and obsidian and were flaked by pressure.

without his chipping kit, a pad of sagebrush bark, a flat piece of tree bark or some green moss would serve in place of the leather pad. The horn would be substituted by using a bone or a tooth fragment set in a wooden handle. A hardwood stick or a sliver of rock will often do the job, though not as well. The ability to improvise cannot be underestimated for the variety of techniques in working stone.

Pecking or Crumbling

The shaping of stones by crumbling requires relatively little brain power. The main requirements are perseverance and a resignation to monotony. The nervous breaking point was probably often reached by the caveman who shattered his newly finished axehead with that final perfectionist's tap. One can almost hear the canyons ringing with whatever verbal abuses entered the primitive mind way back then.

The king of stone-working implements, the hammerstone, is all that is needed here. With it, plus infinite patience, can be shaped colossal stelae and monumental blocks of solid stone for temples. However, primitive man, for the most part, was content to use the simple hammerstone for making axes, clubheads, mortars and pestles, metates and manos and various other necessary items. (Figure 139.) Hammerstones are best made from quartzite cobbles and may have a variety of shapes and sizes. To use them it is only necessary to start pecking away at another rock, preferably one that is slightly softer than the hammerstone. The strokes should be even and rapid, not too hard, and kept up until the surface of the stone being shaped starts to crumble away into a fine dust. The rock being shaped should never rest on a solid surface as it will crack under the blows of the hammerstone. It is preferably held loosely in the hand. In this way the tool slowly takes shape. The crumbling process is speeded up if water is added to the crumbling surface. (Figure 140.) Axes are generally roughly shaped by percussion flaking with the hammerstone prior to being submitted to the crumbling process. The final sharpening and polishing is done by the abrading process. A good axehead can be turned out in about one hour. Another hour of grinding and polishing will give it the touch of beauty found in the finest of southwestern stone work.

Axes are easily hafted by heating a slender willow and wrapping it twice around the axehead. The willow is held in place by wrapping it with willow shoots or cord. This method is not matched for efficiency and ease of handling. The handle will hold tightly and withstand much abuse. (Figure 141.)

Abrading Process

Grinding, cutting, sawing, drilling, scraping, whetting, rasping and polishing are all part of the abrading process. The use of abrasion is

Fig. 139. Making a metate (grinding stone) by pecking with a hafted hammerstone.

Fig. 140. Using a hammerstone to peck a groove for hafting a stone hammer.

Fig. 141. Hafting axeheads in this manner is unequaled for simplicity and utility.

important in shaping and finishing stones used in food preparation. The smoothing of grinding implements reduces much of the grit content in foodstuffs. The cutting edges of implements made of granular stones such as basalt and slate are honed to perfection by abrasion.

Grinding and whetting of stone simply requires another stone upon which the implement is rubbed. The best abrading stones are sandstone and other granular rocks that contain hard grains of silica. Sand is often used as an abrasive, being poured on the surface of the abrading stone. The use of water to step up the process is effective. Even the hardest agates may be ground and polished by rubbing and simple abrasion. Like the crumbling process, it takes time and patience. With the exception of the honing of cutting edges and smoothing food-grinding implements, grinding and polishing of stone are largely for giving a finished look to tools that are already serviceable.

Cutting or sawing of stone is accomplished not with a toothedged stone saw but by simple abrasion with thin slabs of an abrasive stone. Jade and other tough materials are beautifully carved and grooved with simple slab saws using sand and water as abrasive agents.

Drilling of stone is done in a number of ways. The most common method is a pump drill with a stone bit. The bit is necessarily made of very hard material, jasper and agate being the finest. With a good pump drill it is a simple matter to drill slate, chert, basalt, ryolite, or any other soft stone. With the addition of fine quartz sand as an abrasive, even hard stone may in time be penetrated. Water added to the work in most forms of drilling speeds up the work but must be repeatedly replenished and the hole cleaned out to keep the grit dust from forming a thick paste and choking up the drill. (Figure 142.)

Other simple drills include a simple stick drill with a stone bit. This device is twirled between the hands. The simplest drill is merely a bit grasped in the fingers and twisted back and forth into the material being drilled. (Figure 143.)

Stone bits are usually required to get the hole started. After a shallow hole is formed in the stone, the bit may be substituted with bone or hardwood with sand as an abrasive. The bone or wood grips the grains of sand and causes them to cut rapidly into the stone. Water cannot be used with a wooden drill bit as it causes the wood to swell and bind.

Stone Versus Steel

The utility of stone tools as compared to modern ones of metal leaves little doubt as to which is superior. At the same time stone cannot be regarded as totally inferior. It has been noted that flint arrow points are entirely on par with steel heads in penetrating power. Stone axeheads, though somewhat slower, will cut down a tree with as much sureness as the finest steel axe. A stone drill bit will make as neat a hole as a high carbon steel one, and a flint knife will skin a deer and cut it up just as well as any modern butcher's sword.

Thus, it seems reasonable to a few dedicated Stone Age artisans that a mastery of the techniques of the Stone Age is imperative to true outdoor survival. To the other "assumption consumers" it is fitting to leave them awed while their closest friends with utter conviction explain to them that the Indians made arrowheads with fire and a wet straw.

Fig. 142. Using a pump drill with a stone bit.

Fig. 143. Hand drilling with a stone-tipped drill.

Bone Working

Cutting and carving bones into useful implements presents some special problems when working with stone tools only. A few tips on handling bone-working implements will greatly reduce the time and sweat required to make a simple bone tool.

1. Splitting bones. The tool of value here is a graver. This is made by flaking a small nipple on the edge of a piece of hard stone, preferably agate or jasper. It is used to scratch a light groove down the length of the bone. Using the groove as a guide channel, the cut is deepened by stroking rapidly with the graver tip. The process is repeated on the opposite side of the bone. The bone is then split by laying it on a stone and tapping it with a small rock. The tapping is repeated all along the edges of the grooves until the bone splits. (Figures 144 and 145.)

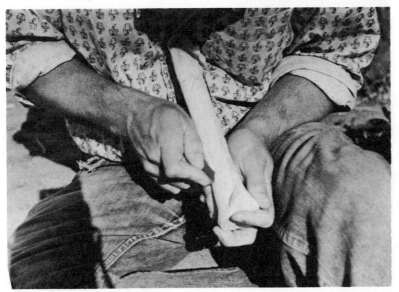

Fig. 144. Splitting bone with a graver.

2. Notching bones. Sometimes a bone tool needs notches for tying on strings or for jagged cutting edges. These are carved with a stone flake. (Figure 146.)
3. Sharpening and honing bone. This is done with a sanding stone. (Figure 147.) The bone is rubbed back and forth on a rough stone surface and finished on a finer sanding stone.

144

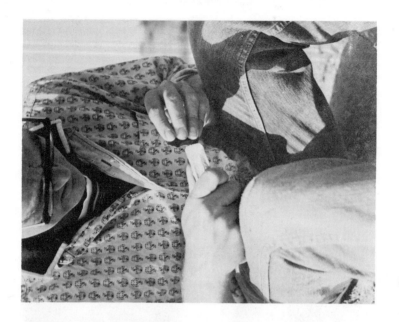

Fig. 146. Cutting notches in bone with a stone flake.

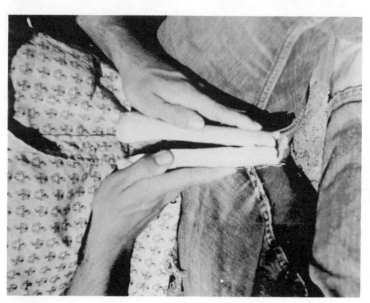

Fig. 145. Bone split with a graver.

Small pieces of bone that need grinding may be placed between two sanding surfaces and the top one rubbed back and forth on the bottom one. The bone between them will be ground rapidly.

4. Drilling bones. The processes for drilling bones is exactly the same as that described for drilling stone. (See "Stone Working," p. 141.)

Bows and Arrows

An archer under primitive conditions is somewhat different from the modern bowman with his laminated finery. His equipment even at best is vastly inferior and unmatched. His success in hunting depends more on infinite patience, practice, good luck and a keen stalking ability that allows him close shots at game. Even with these limitations, a bow is an important aid in filling the stewpot. The perfect shot quite often presents itself in the wilderness, and it is the wise hunter who has something to take the shot with. (Figure 148.)

Making a "quickie" bow for immediate use is usually the concern of a person lost in the wilds. By following a few important steps, this operation can be accomplished in a few hours.

The finest woods for a bow include mountain mahogany *(Cercocarpus)*, ash *(Fraxinus)*, service berry *(Amelanchier)*, and chokecherry *(Prunus)*. A sapling burned by a brush fire is excellent bow wood. Many trees have been uprooted by wind and have well-seasoned branches. A dead tree with its roots still in the ground may be too brittle or weather split for use unless killed by fire. Green wood must be cured.

A long smooth and straight branch about the size of a man's wrist, free of knots or cracks, should be selected. The piece is then shaped into a bow by adzing with a stone adz blade and then by scraping with a sharp, angular chip of stone. (Figure 149.) The belly side is scraped flat, leaving the rounded outside or sapwood for the back of the bow. The back should not be worked down except where heavy knots interfere with the bow's draw. Even then the knots are not made level with the rest of the back but rather are smoothed and rounded to conform with the natural grain of the wood.

Measurements for a bow depend on the individual. By holding the stave diagonally across the chest with one hand at the hip and the other extended straight out to the side at shoulder level, the length of the bow is established. This is normally around 44 inches. The dimensions at the handgrip should be around 5/8" x 1 1/2" and the limbs at the middle should be about 9/16" x 1 7/8". The tips should measure about 5/16" x 3/4".

146

Fig. 147. Sharpening a bone awl on a grooved piece of sandstone.

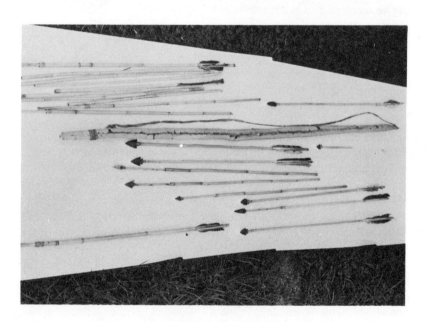

Fig. 148. Primitive bow and arrows made by the author.

Fig. 149. Adzing a staff for a bow. The adze is made of a fine-grained basalt rock.

The final smoothing of the bow is accomplished by rubbing with a piece of fine sandstone. A bow can be strengthened and improved by recurving the ends. This is done by greasing the ends with the fat of an animal and heating them over hot coals or a hot rock. After one end is thoroughly heated—not scorched—it is bent by forcing it around the knee. The bow is held in this position until it cools. The final step is to wrap the ends down about four inches with sinew and allow the bow to season at least a day. (Figure 150.)

Bowstrings

The strongest bowstrings are made from sinew. (See "Sinew Preparation," p. 168.) Nettle, milkweed and some barks are inferior but usable substitutes. The length of the string should be at least twelve inches longer than the bow.

148

Sinew strands are twisted together in the following manner: Holding two strands of sinew in the left hand pinched together between the thumb and second joint of the forefinger, the strand that is farthest from the body is twisted clockwise with the right hand and then folded back *over* the second strand counterclockwise. This puts the second strand in the outside position to be twisted and brought back over the first one in the same manner. This process is continued until the required length is achieved. Splicing new length to the cord is done by carefully laying it alongside the last inch of the cord strand and twisting the two together. If care is taken to taper the ends for splicing, the diameter of the cord will not be increased. (Figures 151, 152, 153, 154, and 155.)

A sinew string is finished by stretching it between two points and rubbing saliva into it until all the rough spots are smoothed down. It must dry in this position.

Arrows

Serviceable arrow shafts may be produced in several ways. Since feathers are a premium in a wilderness situation, arrows may be made without them. When feathers are available, glue for fletching them may be lacking. With these limitations, one can see that methods of arrow production used under primitive conditions are vastly different from those used at home. Also the end products will differ in many ways.

Arrows without fletchings are made from light woods and reeds. Common river reed *(Phragmites Communis)* is the first choice. Willow *(Salix)* and a variety of light pithy woods can be used when reeds are not available. (Figure 156.)

Reeds suitable for arrows are cut when dry. The length of each shaft should be about 24 inches, with the cuts made one-half inch above a joint on the nock end and three or four inches below a joint on the tip end. This allows a strong place for the nock to be cut and leaves a hollow tube at the other end to receive a foreshaft. A reed shaft is straightened by rubbing grease on the joints if available and holding it over hot coals or on a hot rock until heated and then lightly bending it until straight. It must be held in this position until cooled. Reed stems are difficult to straighten between the joints, and care must be taken not to break them at this point. They can rarely be completely straightened. Sinew is wrapped around the tip end to keep it from splitting. The nock is cut at the top and wrapped with sinew for added strength.

Foreshafts are cut from any heavy hardwood tree or brush. They are cut in six to eight inch lengths, sharpened and hardened in the fire with a point on one end and blunted on the other. The blunt tip is inserted into the hollow end of the reed stem and the arrow is complete.

Fig. 150. Shooting a quickie bow made from a dry chokecherry stave. The belly was flattened by hacking and scraping with stone tools and the back was left natural. The string is made of sinew. Note the peculiar style of shooting which is a type formerly used by some Yana Indian groups.

Fig. 151. The proper position for holding two strands of sinew.

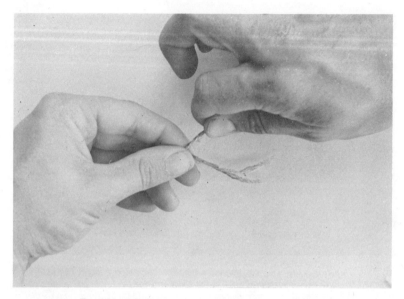

Fig. 152. Twisting the strands in a clockwise direction.

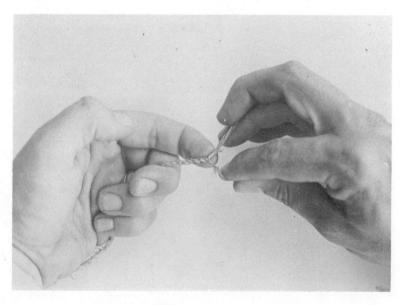

Fig. 153. Folding the twisted strand over the top of the other strand.

Fig. 154. Splicing on another strand.

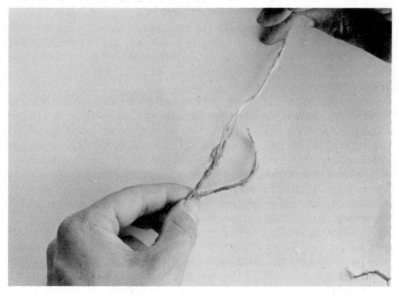

Fig. 155. The splice is completed by twisting the strands together.

Fig. 156. Arrows made from reeds (phragmites). *The foreshafts are of hardwood.*

These flimsy arrows are best used with a lightweight bow and prove effective for flock shooting and small game. A dozen or more of them can be made in one evening around the fire. They may only last for a few shots, but the simplicity and speed in which they are constructed makes them important and effective arrows. These same reed shafts can be made more accurate and deadly by the addition of stone points and fletchings. (Figure 157.)

Woods best suited for sturdy hunting arrows are chokecherry *(Prunus)*, serviceberry *(Amelanchier)*, rose *(Rosa)*, currant *(Ribes)* and willow *(Salix)*. The shafts are selected from young shoots found growing in shaded areas where they must grow tall and straight to reach the sunlight. After cutting, they are allowed to dry in the sun for one day. The bark is then peeled and the still green shafts are cut into lengths several inches longer than the standard set for the finished arrows. They are then sorted according to size and weight and tied into bundles of five or six and left to dry slowly in the shade for two days. The drying process can be speeded up by allowing sunlight to dry them or by holding them over hot coals. The danger of splitting is increased when quick drying is used. However, effective arrow shafts can be turned out within a few hours after cutting by drying with heat. Only after the shafts are completely dry can they be made into arrows. If arrows are made in groups of five at a time (completing each step with all five before going on) much time is saved and the arrows will be better matched for more accurate shooting.

Straightening the shafts is simple and is done in the same manner described for straightening cane shafts. Simply heat the crooked part and work it out over the knee or with the fingers. An arrow wrench for taking out difficult crooks is effective. This is made by drilling a hole in a flat bone and using it to "pry" out the crooks. An even quicker method is to use the teeth. The shaft is gripped just below the crook and wrenched straight with the hands. (Figures 158 and 159.)

When the shafts are completely straight and dry they are scraped down and smoothed with a chip of stone or broken glass. By scraping lengthwise the shafts are made round and even. If a stone tip is to be used, the nock for the bowstring should be at the large end of the shaft. If the point is going to be simply sharpened and hardened in the fire, the nock should be made in the small end. Nocking the shaft for the bowstring is done by sawing with a sharp chip of stone. The nock should be U-shaped and about one-quarter inch deep.

Fletching an arrow by hand is not difficult if glue is used. The feathers are bound in place until the glue dries and the ends of the feathers are secured with sinew. Animal glue is made by boiling down fish skins or hooves. Some plants contain a sticky sap. Pine pitch and plant saps, however, are not good fletching materials.

Since animal glue is hard to make, fletching without glue often becomes necessary in the wilderness. To accomplish this, long feathers are selected from the same wing or the same side of the tail. They are then split with a fine chip of obsidian or other sharp stone. The excess spine can be scraped away in the following manner: The maker sits on the ground and holds one end of the feather on a smooth rock with his big toe, stretches it taut with his left hand and scrapes away the excess spine with a sharp stone chip. A little practice will enable a person to prepare feathers with professional accuracy.

The feathers are then all cut to the same length, from four to six inches, and the web is stripped off for one inch at the base. They are attached to the shaft in the following manner:

1. Measure the point on the shaft that the web of the feather will reach when fully fletched.
2. From that point measure up the shaft toward the *nock* about one inch or the distance from the tip of the stripped quill to the beginning of the web.
3. Place one feather on the shaft upside down and inverted so that the tip of the base is even with the one inch mark on the shaft.
4. Bind the stripped end of the feather to the shaft in this position using only one or two wraps of sinew.
5. Lay on the other two feathers in the proper position and bind all of them down tightly with sinew in the same manner.
6. Lift each feather, bending the quill at the point where the web

154

Fig. 158. The crooks are worked out of a shaft by heating it and bending it over the knee.

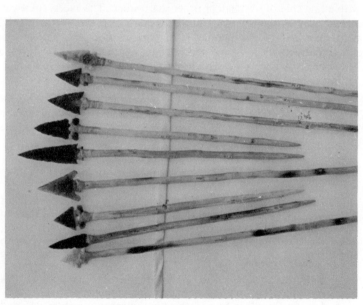

Fig. 157. Stone tipped foreshafts for cane arrows.

Fig. 159. Using an arrow wrench or shaft straightener.

starts, and lay them flat against the shaft. The tips on the top end of the feathers are not stripped but lightly ruffled back and dampened with the fingers to hold them out of the way. Sinew is wrapped over the ends just below the nock, leaving enough feather tip sticking out to grasp with the fingers.

7. Grasp each tip with the fingers or with an improvised pair of pinchers and pull them tight. This flattens the quill against the shaft and stiffens the vane.

8. Wrap on additional sinew to secure the feathers tightly. Allow the sinew to dry and trim off the excess with a stone chip. (Figures 160, 161, 162, 163, 164, 165, 166, 167 and 168.)

Attaching the Points

Filing a notch to receive a stone or bone point is hard work without

156

a steel knife. It is much easier to "break out" a notch by using an old trick:

1. A notch is cut on each side of the shaft at the point where the shaft length is determined to be. (It will be remembered that the shaft was previously cut several inches longer than required.)
2. Another notch is cut on each side of the shaft between the first two notches one-quarter of an inch above them on the shaft.
3. When submitted to gentle pressure and bending, the excess shaft will break off, leaving a deep notch in the end to receive the head. (Figure 169.)

Before fitting the point to the shaft, the notch should be smoothed and sanded to fit the contour of the point and the rough edges removed. The point is inserted in the notch, wrapped on with sinew and, if possible, glued with pitch. When the sinew is dry, the arrow is complete and ready for use. (Figure 170.)

Atlatl and Spear

A simple but effective weapon for large game is called an atlatl. This device predates the bow and arrow and was used anciently to hunt large game. The Australian aborigines, Eskimos and some Mexican Indians still

Fig. 160. Feathers are scraped in this manner to thin down the quill for good fletching.

157

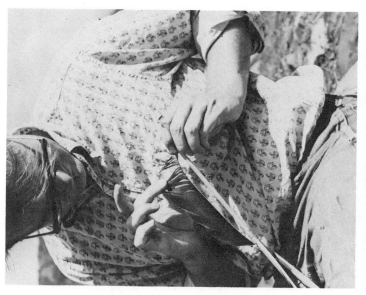

Fig. 162. The tips are lightly ruffled back and dampened to hold them out of the way.

Fig. 161. Feathers wrapped on the shaft in an inverted position. They are then bent back toward the nock end of the shaft.

158

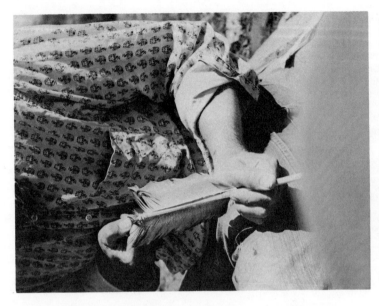

Fig. 164. Each tip is pulled to flatten the quill against the shaft.

Fig. 163. The tips are tied on the shaft with sinew.

Fig. 165. Tail end of feathers bound with sinew. Note that the wrapping not only binds the quills but also some of the web. This helps secure the feathers tightly so they will not slip after rough use.

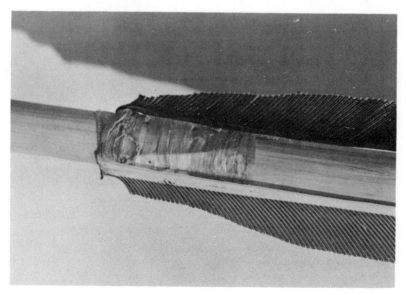

Fig. 166. The folded ends are pulled firmly back when the other ends are pulled. This will not allow the fletchings to work loose in time.

160

Fig. 167. The excess web is cut off with a stone flake by laying the web on a piece of wood and drawing the blade evenly along the web.

Fig. 168. Completed arrow.

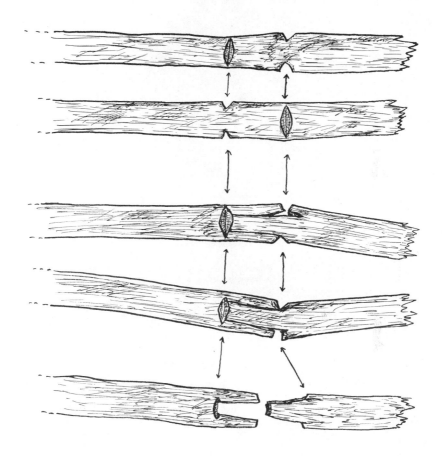

Fig. 169. Breaking out a notch.

Fig. 170. A hafted point.

use them. The atlatl is a stick used to throw a light spear or dart with greater force and distance than is possible with just the arm. It acts as a lengthening of the arm, thus giving greater power to the thrower.

The atlatl is about two feet long, two inches wide and one-half inch thick. A prong is carved at one end to fit into the hollow butt of the spear, and two loops are tied at the other end through which the fingers of the thrower are passed. (Figure 171.)

The spear or dart is about five or six feet long with a foreshaft of hardwood about six inches long, tipped with a stone point. The butt end is hollowed to receive the prong of the atlatl. Two feathers are tied to the sides near the butt end to help balance the spear in flight. The spear shaft may be made of willow or any straight sapling. A young straight juniper

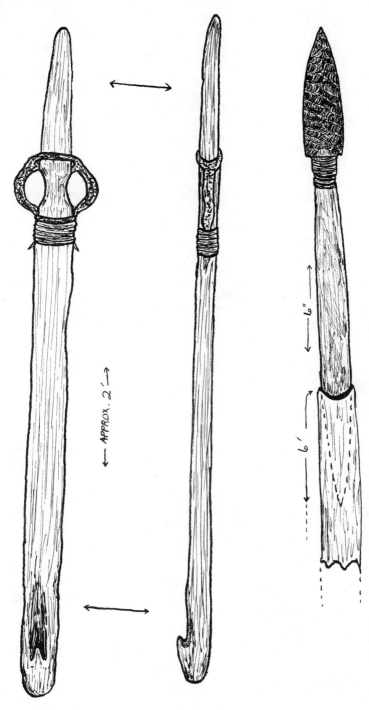

← APPROX. 2' →

6"

6'

Fig. 171. Atlatl or throwing board and details of foreshaft for the spear. The finger loops on the atlatl are made of leather or cordage and bound with sinew or strong fiber.

shoot is excellent but rare. Pine saplings found growing in dense thickets are sometimes straight and slender. Any shaft can be straightened by heating and bending. The finished spear should be slender—not too heavy or cumbersome. A hole is drilled in the tip end to receive the foreshaft. Cord is wrapped around the drilled end to keep it from splitting on impact. The feathering of the shaft need not be elaborate. Simply tie two feathers securely at both ends and at the middle. The following pointers will aid in the construction of the atlatl and spear.

1. A natural bump or twig may be utilized for the prong on the atlatl.
2. The wood is carved and shaped, using stone tools as described under "Arrow Making," p. 148.
3. Drilling wood is best done with a stone or bone drill set in the ground or held between the feet and the shaft twirled on it by spinning it between the palms of the hands.

Using the atlatl with skill demands much practice. Blunt spears without foreshafts should be used for practice and for small game. (Figure 172.) When throwing the spear, it should be remembered that a snapping powerful throw is not necessary. The spear should be thrown overhanded with a sweeping even motion. The spear should be thrown straight at the target and not lopped over to it. When the butt end of the spear tends to dip down, thus spoiling its flight, it is a sign that the thrower is flipping it too hard or that the spear is too heavy. (Figures 173, 174 and 175.)

Cordage

Materials
Strange as it may seem, a piece of string may become the most important item in a survival situation. Practically everything requires this simple item that we hardly think about at home. Equally strange is the simplicity with which it can be manufactured in nature. Anything from sewing thread to hanging ropes can be made from a number of common wayside plants. The following is a breakdown of the common fibers and what can be best made from each:

1. Stinging Nettle, *Urtica*
   Uses: the stalks contain a silky fiber that is very strong. The dried stalks are pounded to remove the woody parts and fiber is cleaned by hand. It can be used to make thread, fish line, string, yarn, snares, nets, ropes, cloth, bowstrings, sandals, blankets, woven sacks, etc.
2. Milkweed, *Asclepias*
   Uses: The stalks contain a silky fiber that can be used when the plant is green or dry. It is best harvested dry. It is processed in the same way as nettle and may serve the same purposes.

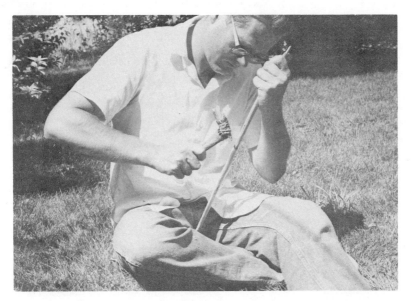

Fig. 172. Adzing a piece of wood to be made into an atlatl.

Fig. 173. Proper position for holding the spear in the atlatl.

Fig. 174. The spear should be thrown overhanded in this position.

Fig. 175. The aim should be directly at the game with a steady overhand flip.

3. Dogbane, *Apocynum cannabinum*
   Uses: This plant is perhaps the best fiber plant found in the West. The stalks contain a fine soft silky fiber that is easily worked. It is processed the same as nettle and milkweed and serves the same uses.

4. Haw, Hawthorn or Thornapple, *Crataegus*
   Uses: The inner white bark of this food tree is usable as cordage. It will not serve the multitude of uses of the fiber plants listed above but can be stripped and twisted into effective string and rope. It will serve in a pinch for fish line, snares and sandals. The bark is strongest when wet and becomes a little stiff when dry. Other trees having similar barks for cordage are willow, elm, spruce roots, rose and snowberry.

5. Sagebrush, *Artemisia tridentata*
   Uses: The dry bark is stripped from the trunks and twisted into cordage. This bark is not strong but has a wide variety of uses. It may be made into coarse woven bags and blankets. It is the principal cordage for making sandals. The rope made from it is not very strong but will serve for tying things together and for holding timbers in position for shelters. It may be pounded and used for tinder. Other plants that have similar bark are juniper trees and cliffrose *(Cowania)*. The barks of all these plants can be gathered in large quantities and used for bedding and thatching materials.

Twisting Cordage

The process of hand twisting cordage is as follows:

1. Two strips of fiber are selected and held in the left hand between the thumb and forefinger.
2. The fiber farthest from the body is grasped in the fingers of the right hand and twisted clockwise.
3. The twisted strand is then laid over the other strand. This places it closest to the body.
4. The second strand (now farthest from the body) is twisted and laid over the first strand in the same manner. This is continued until the ends of the strands are reached.
5. When the ends are reached, other lengths of fiber are spliced on by twisting together the last two inches of the ends to the new fibers and continuing the process of twisting and folding. It is best to alternate the lengths of the strands so that the splices do not both come at the same place in the finished string. (Figure 176.)

When short lengths of string are needed for tying something or sewing a few stitches, there is a quick way to produce them by simply holding one end of a long strand in the left hand and rolling it in one direction on the thigh with the right hand. When it is rolled tight, one end is grasped in each hand and the middle is taken in the teeth. The two ends are put together and held tight. Then the end that is in the teeth is allowed to drop and the string will twine together automatically from the tension produced when twisted and rolled on the thigh. This leaves a two-ply cord half the length of the original strand.

Sinew Preparation

The long tendons from the legs of animals and the longer ones from the backs can be prepared and fashioned into cordage that is unequaled in strength. Bowstrings are best made from sinew. (See "Bowstrings," p. 147.) The simple strands also serve to haft arrow points and other tools to their wooden counterparts. They are wrapped on while wet and do not need to be tied since the sinew is sticky enough to glue itself.

When the tendons are taken from the animal, they should be cleaned and placed in the sun until they are completely hard and dry. Then they are placed on a smooth rock and pounded with another rock until they are soft and fluffy white. The sinew will then strip arpart into fine threads. It can be used dry, for sewing thread, or twisted into cords. It can be moistened for use in wrapping and hafting stone implements. (Figure 177.)

Weaving

Like anything else that is worth while, weaving takes time. A number of useful items can be made by using the simple "plain" weave. This over-and-under technique takes little time. Cattail and bulrish stems produce good mats for floor coverings, beds and shelter covers. (Figure 178.)

Twining is another method of weaving that is used to make blankets, bags, sandals, fish traps and some baskets. The foundation strands are called the "warp" and the interwoven strands are called the "weft." There are two weft strands in twining, one going over the warp and the other under it. They are crossed between each warp.

Most baskets for carrying and harvesting seeds and for water bottles are made by the coiled technique. With this, a basket is built up from the base by a growing spiral coil consisting of two small rods of willow and a bundle of fibrous material, usually grass or bark. Each coil is stitched to the one below with a thin splint of willor or bark. The splint is passed through the coil with the aid of a bone awl. (Figure 179.)

169

Fig. 177. Sinew is prepared by pounding a tendon between two smooth stones until it separates into fine threads.

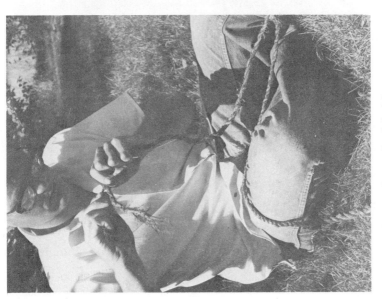

Fig. 176. Twisting sagebrush bark into rope.

170

Fig. 178. Plain weave.

A few pointers to follow when weaving are:

1. Grasses and reeds selected for weaving should be dry and not green.
2. The dried material should be soaked and kept pliable during the weaving process.
3. Willow weaving materials should be cut green and stripped, left to dry and then soaked when used.
4. Splints are made by peeling the bark from willows and then splitting out the outside layer of the wood. The inside core is used for the foundation rods, and the outside or sap wood is used for the splints. Other materials like flat bark strips and rush strips may be used for splints.

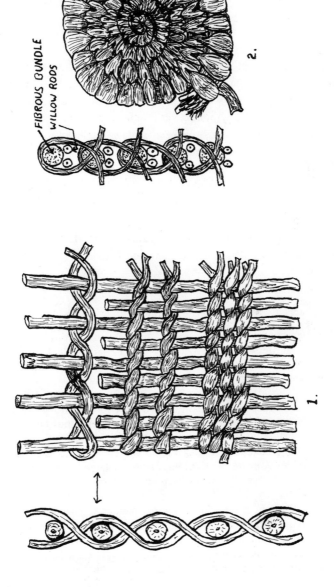

FIBROUS BUNDLE

WILLOW RODS

2.

1.

Fig. 179. (1) Twined weaving. (2) Coiled weaving.

Water jugs are coiled baskets with small openings at the top. They are lined with pitch. The pitch is smeared on the inside before the constricting top is made. The remainder is pitched by placing a lump of pitch inside with a hot rock and shaking the container until the pitch has melted and spread over the surface. Pine pitch is prepared by boiling lumps for about 15 minutes and then skimming off the surface with a flat stick. It must then be heated for use. Another way is to burn the pitch on a sloping rock. The turpentine will burn away, and the pure pitch will run down the rock to be collected and molded into small balls.

By using a very tight coiled weave, some baskets can be made water tight without the pitch liner. The advantage is that it enables one to boil water by placing hot stones in the basket. This is called stone boiling. Food can also be prepared by boiling with rocks in a skin or paunch.

Large burden sacks, packs, blankets, storage-pit liners, clothing and sandals are made from the inner soft bark of the cedar, sagebrush, and cliffrose plants. The strips are fluffed and slightly twisted for the warp strands. Cords and flat strips are used for the weft. A loose twined weave is sufficient for the burden sacks and packs. Sandals are easily made from bark. Time does not usually permit refinement of sandal making, but serviceable ones can be twined in about three hours. They will last for about three days of moderate use. (Figures 180, 181, 182, 183, 184 and 185.)

Making Rawhide

Good rawhide requires a little more care than just letting a green hide dry stiff. Several steps must be taken to render it usable for moccasin soles, bags, pails, ropes, boxes and a number of other utilitarian items. The complete process of making good rawhide is as follows:

1. The hide is soaked in water a day or more if it has previously been dried out. If the hide is green this step is not taken.
2. The hide is staked out with the flesh side up, and a flesher is used to scrape and hack off all the fat and excess tissue. The flesher is made from a long bone of a large animal. One side is honed down to a very sharp edge and small teeth are cut in it. A strap is fastened to the top to serve as a wrist support. The instrument is used in a hacking manner to peel and scrape the fat from the hide. Stone scrapers are held in the hand and used in a drawing motion across the hide. (Figures 186 and 187.)
3. The hide is washed and cleaned and left staked out to dry in the sun for a couple of days. During the washing process the

Fig. 180. Examples of twined weaving.

Fig. 181. Starting of a bark blanket using twined weaving.

174

Fig. 182. Bark blankets may be used for keeping warm when nothing else is available.

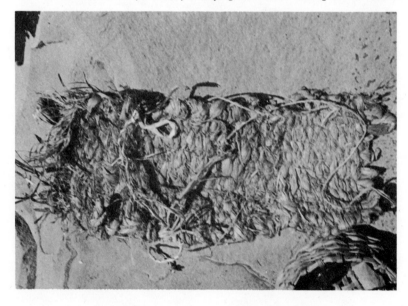

Fig. 183. Sagebrush bark sandal made by twining.

Fig. 184. Sandal made from cattail leaves by twining.

Fig. 185. Example of coiled weaving.

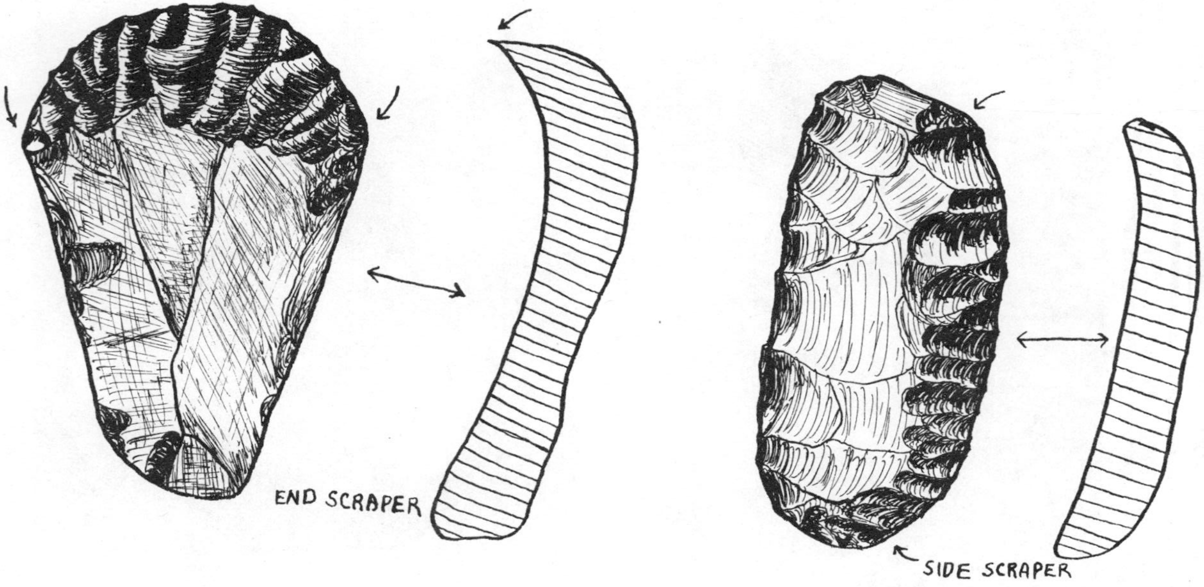

176

Fig. 186. Stone scrapers.

scrapers should be used to make sure all fat is removed. Water is normally used for this, but better results can be achieved by using urine. Though this may be upsetting to most people, it still stands proven as a superior way of cleaning a hide. It is allowed to soak into the hide until the fat is all dissolved by the strong acids. It is then scraped off, taking the fats with it. The urine cleaning is followed by a good washing with water.

4. After the hide is dry and stiff, the stakes are removed and the hide is turned over and restaked. Using a hair scraper, all the hair is removed by scraping with a sideways motion and covering every inch of the hide. This is back breaking work, but it can be somewhat easier if the hide is soaked in wood ashes overnight. This loosens the hair and lets it slip out instead of being shaved off by the hair scraper. Hair scrapers are simply small hoes made of wood, bone or horn. A sharp stone blade is attached to the hoe end. These blades must be resharpened frequently. (Figure 188.)

5. The final step in making rawhide is to place the dry hide on a soft pad of grass or old blankets and to pound it with a blunt stone hammer weighing about three or four pounds. The hide should be struck with short glancing blows. Every inch of the hide must be covered to break the grain and make it white and soft. Rawhide prepared this way is almost as soft as tanned shoe leather and just as tough.

Tanning

Lightweight skins are tanned easily with or without the hair on. Animals with hollow hair, such as deer, antelope, moose and elk, must have the hair removed. Tanning does not set the hair of these animals in the hide and they continually shed. The hair is scraped or slipped off in the same manner as described under "Making Rawhide," and the hide is put through the same process of soaking and scraping off the flesh. Light skins like deer and elk do not require the whitening or pounding process as described for making rawhide.

The tanning agent used is the brain from the animal providing the hide or any other brain. Generally speaking, one deer brain will tan one deer hide and one mouse brain will tan one mouse hide. The time lapse involved from the moment of the kill until the hide is ready for tanning may be considerably longer than most brains remain fresh. They can be preserved for use by lightly cooking and sealing them in a section of intestine. This is a very necessary precaution since there is nothing quite like "ripe" brains.

When the hide is ready for tanning, it should be staked out dry. The warmed brains are mashed fine and rubbed on the skin with a smooth stone until they completely saturate it. The skin is then rolled up and placed in a warm place overnight. The next day the skin is staked out and scraped thoroughly to remove all excess brain tissue. It is then worked back and forth through a rope loop. This friction dries it, finishing the tanning process.

If the hide is intended for clothing or moccasins, it should be smoked. This allows the leather to dry soft again if it gets wet. It is done by forming the skin around a tripod under which is built a tiny smudge fire. This tepee arrangement allows the smoke to penetrate the skin quickly. The longer it is smoked the darker becomes the color. A light buckskin brown indicates the skin is smoked just right.

Fig. 187. Scraping a deerskin with a bone scraper.

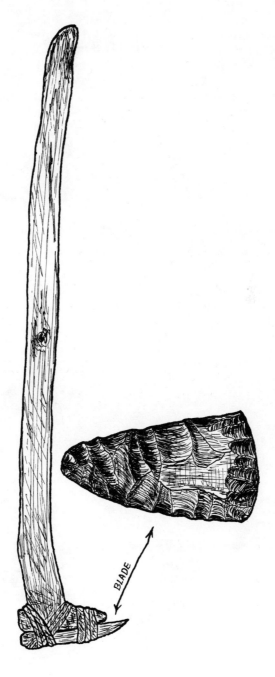

BLADE

Fig. 188. Half scraper.

180

— NOTES —

INDEX

Greens: as food, 38
Grinding: of stones, 140
Grinding stones, 38
Ground Cherry, 61
Ground squirrels: fooling of, 111
Grubs, 94

Hafting: arrowpoints, 155; axe
    heads, 139
Hairgrass, 61
Hair scraper, 177
Hammerstone, 131, 138
Hand drill, see Fire making
Handstone, see Metate and Mano
Hardening wood: in fire, 34
Hardwood: coals for parching,
    drills, 141; fish spear prongs,
    114; for digging sticks, 34;
    use in fire making, 21
Haw: bark as cordage, 167; bark
    as fish line, 113; berries as
    food, see Thornapple
Hawks Beard, 62
Hawthorn, see Thornapple
Headache: as defense against
    eating, 34; treatment for, 91
Heating: ground for bed, see Hot
    pit bed
Heating pit: for sweat lodge shel-
    ter, 10
Heartburn, 91
Helgramites, 94, 124
Helianthus, 87, 82; H. tuberosus,
    64
Hinge fractures, 131
Horehound, see Mint
Horn baton, 131, 134
Horn flaker, 134
Horsemint, see Mint
Horsetail, 62
Hot pit bed, 14, 15
Hot rocks: for heating, 10
Hunting and Stalking, 110
Husk Tomato, see Ground Cherry
Hydrocyanic acid: poison in Arrow-
    grass, 45

Hydrophyllum capitatum, 86
Hyssop, see Mint

Idaho: southern, 2
Indian Lettuce, see Miner's Lettuce
Indian Potato, 63
Indian Ricegrass, 63
Indian Tobacco, see Sour Dock
Indifference: as excuse for not
    eating, 34
Inflamation, 93
Insecticide, 91
Insect repellent, 92
Insects: as food, 94
Insulated Wattle Work, see Shelter

Jackson, Ray D., 29
Jarbridge area of Idaho, 3
Jasper, 131; for drill bits, 141
Jerky, 124
Jerusalem Artichoke, 64
Joint Grass, see Horsetail
Juniper bark: as bedding, 14; as
    cordage, 167, in shelter con-
    struction, 6; in storage pits,
    43; see also Bark, juniper
Juniper: as bow wood, 145; as
    spear, 162; berries as food,
    see Cedar
Juniperus, 57; see also Juniper
Justification for killing game, 94

Knife: flint for skinning, 141
Knowledge of plant life, 34
Kouse, see Biscuitroot

Lactuca, 72
Lamb's Quarter, 64
Large game, 95
Leaching of plant foods, 39
Lean-to, see Shelters
Leather pad used in stone working,
    131, 134
Lewis and Clark: sought bread of
    kouse, 48
Lithic arts, 129